Reading for the Gifted Student

Challenging Activities for the Advanced Learner

Written by **Melissa Gough**

Illustrations by **Remy Simard**

An imprint of Sterling Children's Books

Published by Sterling Publishing Co., Inc.
387 Park Avenue South, New York, NY 10016
Text and illustrations © 2005 by Flash Kids
Distributed in Canada by Sterling Publishing
c/o Canadian Manda Group, 165 Dufferin Street
Toronto, Ontario, Canada M6K 3H6
Distributed in the United Kingdom by GMC Distribution Services
Castle Place, 166 High Street, Lewes, East Sussex, England BN7 1XU
Distributed in Australia by Capricorn Link (Australia) Pty. Ltd.
P.O. Box 704, Windsor, NSW 2756, Australia

Sterling ISBN 978-1-4114-3431-8

Manufactured in Canada

Lot #:
4 6 8 10 9 7 5 3
08/12

For information about custom editions, special sales, premium and
corporate purchases, please contact Sterling Special Sales
Department at 800-805-5489 or specialsales@sterlingpublishing.com.

Cover image © Image Source/Getty Images
Cover design and production by Mada Design, Inc.

Whether your student has been identified as gifted and talented or is simply a scholastic overachiever, school-assigned activities may not be challenging enough for him or her. To keep your student engaged in learning, it is important to provide reading activities that quench his or her thirst for information and allow opportunities to exercise critical thinking.

This workbook contains much more than typical reading passages and questions; it does not rely on the assumption that a gifted and talented fifth-grader simply requires sixth-grade work. Instead, the nearly 200 pages of reading passages, comprehension questions, and creative activities are calibrated to match the average reading level, analytical capacity, and subject interest of this specialized group of learners. Specifically, the vocabulary, sentence structure, and length of passages in this grade 5 workbook are set at levels normally appropriate for grades 6 and 7, but the comprehension skills increase in difficulty as the workbook progresses, starting with grade 5 curriculum standards and working through those associated with grade 6. The passages' topics are primarily nonfiction and present concepts, themes, and issues fundamental to all disciplines, including science, social studies, health, and the arts.

Question formats range from multiple choice and short answer to true-or-false, fill-in-the-blank, and much more. Also sprinkled throughout the workbook are creative activities that will encourage your student to write a story or draw a picture. Your student may check his or her work against the answer key near the end of the workbook, or you may wish to review it together, since many questions have numerous possible answers.

Reading, writing, and language skills are essential to any student's academic success. By utilizing this workbook, you are providing your gifted learner an opportunity to seek new challenges and experience learning at an advanced level.

Contents

Pop! Pop! Create!

Sometimes what is inside a package is not nearly as much fun as the stuff that protects it. For some eleven-year-old students throughout the United States, Bubble Wrap was the inspiration for ways to help make people's lives better. Thanks to a contest sponsored by its creator, Bubble Wrap is stirring the imaginations of young inventors and creating an explosion of ingenuity.

Bubble Wrap was invented in 1960 by Sealed Air Corporation of Elmwood Park, New Jersey. Its main purpose has been to safeguard fragile items being mailed from one place to another. The lightweight, puffy plastic sheets cushion the contents of packages and make sure that items arrive in one piece—not in pieces.

Bubble Wrap has also been known to relieve stress and entertain. Many people love to pop the air-filled pockets or make noise as they stomp on the sheets of protective wrap. Recently, Bubble Wrap got a new job: It inspired eleven-year-old Max Wallack, of Natick, Massachusetts, to invent a way to help his grandmother.

Struggling with everyday tasks, Max's grandmother suffered from carpal tunnel syndrome, a condition that occurs when a main nerve in the arm is compressed, or squeezed. In severe cases, like Max's grandmother's, there is pain and weakness in the wrist. Max watched his grandmother suffer intense pain and he decided to do something about it. He invented special wrist cushions and entered the Bubble Wrap Competition for Young Inventors, a contest sponsored by Sealed Air Corporation and open to students in grades 5 through 8.

According to Max, there's nothing better than "resting on air." He spent months sketching designs and building a prototype, or model, of his idea. He lined socks with Bubble Wrap and used elastics and fasteners to keep the wrist cushions in place. After observing his grandmother trying to complete day-to-day tasks while wearing large and awkward splints from her doctor, Max convinced her to try his prototype. Before her surgery, which is a common way to treat carpal tunnel syndrome, the wrist cushions made Max's grandmother feel more comfortable.

Max's Bubble Wrap wrist cushions made him one of 15 semifinalists in the competition. He competed against 1,400 other students from 39 states. Two important rules of the contest are that the invention has to be an original idea and it must use Bubble Wrap. In the spirit of the inventors of Bubble Wrap, organizers believe that the contest promotes resourcefulness and ingenuity. Max, along with the other 14 semifinalists, will receive a $500 U.S. savings bond. The contest has three finalists and a grand prize winner who receives a $10,000 savings bond.

Answer the questions about the reading.

1. A synonym is a word that means the same as another word. What is a synonym for *compressed*?

_____

severe   squeezed   fund   design

2. Describe your own new use for Bubble Wrap. _____

_____

3. Think about how Max feels about his grandmother. What kind of person do you think Max

is? _____

4. Bubble Wrap was invented to ____.
 a. entertain people   **b.** keep food fresh on its way to the grocery store
 c. use in the space program   **d.** protect items being mailed from one place to another

5. Write the main idea of the reading.

_____

_____

6. Two reasons why Sealed Air Corporation sponsors this contest are to ____ and ____.
 a. make money   **b.** encourage creativity in young people
 c. advertise their products   **d.** help get more people to work for them

7. The judges look for _____ when they try to decide which inventions win the

competition.

8. Use the letters in the words *Bubble Wrap* to make a list of smaller words.

_____

9. Use a thesaurus to find other words for *ingenuity*. List them here.

_____

10. If you wanted to enter the Bubble Wrap Competition for Young Inventors, how might you look

for more information? _____

_____

Presidential Pets

Presidents are as animal loving as anyone else. America's first president, George Washington, kept 36 hound dogs and 12 horses. President Abraham Lincoln and First Lady Mary Todd Lincoln allowed their children to have cats, dogs, goats, ponies, pigs, and rabbits for pets. President Calvin Coolidge loved dogs. When Theodore Roosevelt was president, he took care of twelve horses, five dogs, five guinea pigs, two cats, garter snakes, a toad, a pony, two kangaroo rats, a flock of ducks, a flying squirrel, a badger, a pig, and a blue macaw named Eli! President Roosevelt loved animals,

and when he wasn't running the country or spending time with his pets, he was writing about them. During his second term as president, he wrote a bird-watching book. In all shapes and sizes, presidential pets have ranged from elephants to silkworms. But elephants and silkworms are not exactly soft and furry. More recently, presidents have chosen more traditional pets, such as cats and dogs. Some of the most famous pets include Lucky, Millie, Socks, and Miss Beazley. These presidential pets have been in the spotlight almost as much as their owners.

President Ronald Reagan's dog, Lucky, loved to chase news reporters and play hide-and-seek. Every day Lucky would take a two-hour nap in the Oval Office. When President George H. W. Bush was in office from 1989 to 1993, he and his family enjoyed the company of Millie. Millie was a Springer Spaniel and the only White House pet to "author" her own book. She had a litter of puppies while George H. W. Bush was president, and they all were sent to live with good homes. That is, except Ranger. Ranger stayed at the White House to live with the Bush family.

Socks is probably the most famous cat to live in the White House. Owned by President Bill Clinton, Socks napped on the South Lawn and did not get along with the Clinton family's dog, Buddy.

One of the most well-behaved "first pets" is Barney. Barney is a Scottish terrier who belongs to First Lady Laura Bush. Barney was joined by Miss Beazley, a Scottish terrier pup, in 2005. They learned quickly to play together.

You might have thought that the presidents of the United States wouldn't have time for pets. Well, they do!

Answer the questions about the reading.

1. The most well-behaved dog ever to live at the White House was _____.

2. The word *author* is used as a verb in the reading. A synonym for *author* is _____.

    learn   teach   write   manufacture

3. Do you think that presidential pets receive more attention than pets belonging to everyone else? Why or why not?

_____

4. What do you think the phrase *in the spotlight* means? _____

5. Circle the main idea of the reading.
    a. All presidents own animals.   **b.** Presidential pets get special treatment.
    c. Some presidents like cats better than dogs.   **d.** Pets are popular with many presidents.

6. What do you think the best pet for a president would be? Explain why.

_____

7. Facts tell about things that are true. Opinions are how people feel about things. Read the following statements from the reading and circle the opinions.
    a. Lucky loved to chase reporters.
    b. Socks is probably the most famous cat to live in the White House.
    c. Socks napped on the South Lawn.
    d. You might have thought that the presidents of the United States wouldn't have time for pets. Well, they do!

8. How many pets did George Washington own? _____

9. Of the presidents mentioned in the passage, which one owned the most pets?

_____

    Washington   Roosevelt   G. H. W. Bush   Clinton

10. Write a sentence about your pet or about a pet you would like to own.

_____

_____

Read All About It!

Newspaper editors carefully write just the right headline to make their readers want to read a story. Think about the headlines in your newspaper. They are usually a few words and give information about the article in a catchy way.

Write a paragraph about a fictional pet who lives in the White House. Describe something the pet does that would attract the attention of photographers. For example, maybe the President would have to call the fire department to rescue a cat that is stuck in a tree.

After writing, think of a three- to four-word headline that would make people want to read your story.

Headline _____

_____

_____

_____

_____

_____

_____

_____

_____

_____

_____

Be a Bobblehead

Bobblehead dolls are small collectible figures with oversized heads. With just one tap or nudge, their heads bob and nod around on thin springs attached to their plastic bodies. Bobblehead dolls first appeared in the 1950s, and they were characters and sports heroes. Today even Derek Jeter, the New York Yankees shortstop, has his own bobblehead doll.

Pretend that the American Bobblehead Company is holding a contest to choose the next figure they will manufacture. Write a paragraph to the company that describes one person whom you think would make a good bobblehead doll and why. The rules of the contest state that paragraphs must be well written and include a list of accomplishments or reasons why the person you are nominating should win. Try to choose someone who means something to you and has done something that has impacted our world. Underneath, draw a sketch of your bobblehead doll.

I am nominating _____ to be the next bobblehead doll the American Bobblehead Company manufactures because _____

_____

_____

_____

_____

_____

_____

_____

_____

_____

_____

_____

Lunch, Anyone?

Plants that eat insects and spiders seem more like science fiction than scientific fact. But for thousands of years, more than 500 different kinds of plants have been feasting on small creatures. The Venus flytrap is one of them.

Venus flytraps grow along the coast of North and South Carolina. That's the only place in the world where scientists have found the plant growing. Venus flytraps live in wet, sunny bogs and love humidity. They also love spiders and flies.

Most plants survive on water and nutrients from the soil and gases in the air, but Venus flytraps also like to eat bugs. In addition to spiders and flies, these carnivorous plants consume caterpillars, crickets, and slugs. Because the bogs where the Venus flytraps grow lack the kinds of vitamins and nutrients the plants need to live, they must find it elsewhere. So the Venus flytrap catches and eats living creatures.

In order for a plant to be labeled carnivorous, the plant must be able to attract and capture insects. It also must be able to tell the difference between food and what is inedible. The third requirement is that the plant be capable of digesting its prey, or the bug it just caught for food. Plants do not have brains, so all of these things are done through mechanical and chemical processes.

In order to attract insects, the Venus flytrap uses its leaves, which secrete, or produce, a sweet nectar. This sugary juice acts like a magnet, drawing in bugs searching for food. Each leaf is lined with six short and stiff hairs, called trigger hairs. When an insect lands on a leaf and touches one of the hairs, the flytrap senses that something is there. The trigger hairs act like a motion detector. Two hairs must be brushed, one after the other, in order for the plant to close up around the bug.

Scientists aren't exactly sure how the Venus flytrap knows the difference between a spider and a twig that might fall into its trap. Perhaps as the plant's trigger hairs continue to be disturbed by its live food, they close its trap completely. If whatever fell into the trap stops moving, the leaves open approximately twelve hours later. Whatever blew in will blow back out.

Once the bug is locked inside, the plant's leaf acts like a stomach and digests the insect. Depending on the size of the bug, the Venus flytrap needs from five to twelve days to finish its meal.

Answer the questions about the reading.

1. What is the only place where Venus flytraps grow? _____

2. Circle the meaning of *carnivorous*.
    a. an animal or plant that only eats plants   **b.** an animal or plant that only eats living things
    c. a plant that uses the sun as a source for food   **d.** an insect that looks for something to eat

3. Circle the phrases in the box that describe what the Venus flytrap does.

> converts sunlight to food   eats bugs   digests its food in one hour
> completely closes its trap when it senses prey   secretes a sugary substance

4. The Venus flytrap attracts its prey with its _____.

5. Circle all the synonyms for, or words that mean the same as, *feasting* in the word bank.

> eating   devouring   gobbling up   sleeping   consuming   running   resting

6. What do trigger hairs do?

_____

7. If the Venus flytrap knew which human foods are made of meat, which of the following do you
    think it would like? Circle all of your choices.

> lettuce   hamburger   ice cream   pork chop   chicken   oranges

8. The word *secrete* means to _____.

9. Number the events in the correct order.
    _____ The plant closes its leaves.
    _____ A bug sees the Venus flytrap's nectar.
    _____ The bug lands on the leaf.
    _____ Trigger hairs tell the plant that it might be mealtime.
    _____ The Venus flytrap needs up to twelve days to digest its prey.

10. Would you like to own a Venus flytrap? Why or why not?

_____

_____

Mickey Mantle and Me

The only thing I like better than playing baseball is going to watch the Yankees play baseball. I love riding in my Uncle Michael's car. As we're stuck in traffic with my dad and older brother, John, we anticipate an afternoon of hot dogs and some of the best baseball around. The day feels like nothing else in the world. During the game, I lean way over my seat after each play to check that my scorebook looks exactly like Uncle Michael's.

Afterward, we always walk over to Monument Park. As I stand beside Mickey Mantle's plaque, my uncle tells the story we've heard so many times before. "It was a hot August day in 1964," he begins. "The Yankees were playing the White Sox. I saw Mickey hit two home runs that day." Uncle Michael shakes his head and smiles. "That man could hit. Even sitting in the outfield, you could feel the power in his swing."

"One of his friends once said that Mickey swung from the soul," Dad says.

I try to imagine what it might have felt like to see Mickey Mantle play ball. I am sure I know how Mickey felt. Every time I step up to the plate with my bat, I can feel the power building in my swing. It starts at my feet and rises up through my knees and into my arms. Being that strong feels so good.

I am listening and thinking, and then my scorebook slips from my hands. As I reach to pick it up, my hand brushes Mickey's plaque. Suddenly, the grass is gone and I am looking at worn, wooden floorboards. I stand up slowly and see a ballplayer standing in front of me.

"Hey, how'd you get in here?" asks the player.

"I…I don't know," I say. I don't know where I am, but I know that face. It's Mickey Mantle himself.

"Well, center field is waiting for me. How about an autograph while you're here?" he asks. I hand him my book. He asks me what my name is. Then, as he hands the book back, he reaches out to shake my hand. As quickly as I found myself in the old Yankees locker room, I am back with my family.

"You okay, Joe?" asks John. Uncle Michael helps me up. As he passes the scorebook to me, he stops and shows it to Dad first. They both look at each other and then at me. I take the scorebook and look down. It reads: *To Joe, Play from the heart. Mickey Mantle.*

Answer the questions about the story.

1. Who is the author of this story? _____

2. Do you think that Joe admires his Uncle Michael? Circle the sentences in the story that are clues.

3. Where do Joe, John, Dad, and Uncle Michael walk to after every Yankees game they watch?
_____

4. What gives you the impression that Joe is probably a good batter? Underline the sentences that are clues.

5. What position did Mickey Mantle play? _____

6. Circle the sentence that tells you what position he played.

7. How did Joe get into the old Yankees locker room?_____
_____

8. This story is an example of _____.
   a. nonfiction   **b.** historical fiction
   c. a news story   **d.** a persuasive article

9. What do you think Joe's dad and Uncle Michael thought when they saw Joe's scorebook?
_____
_____

10. What do you think will happen next?
_____
_____
_____

Putting the Spin on the Ball

A good curveball can be the difference between a decent baseball pitcher and a great baseball pitcher. With a roll of the fingers, a curveball has been known to frustrate batters and win games.

A curveball is one of the easiest pitches to control. It is a fairly easy pitch to learn, but it goes a long way if performed properly. Invented in the late 1800s, the curveball was considered dishonest and was banned. But baseball officials couldn't stop pitchers from using it.

Many famous baseball players threw curveballs. Sandy Koufax, or the "man with the golden arm," was one of the greatest pitchers in professional baseball. He loved the game and was famous for his curveball. Throughout his career, Koufax broke many pitching records and was elected to the Baseball Hall of Fame in 1972. More recently, pitchers such as Barry Zito and Nolan Ryan have been recognized for both their curveball and pitching accomplishments.

In professional baseball games, the curveball is about 15 miles per hour faster than a fastball. While a fastball has backspin, or a spin that goes in reverse of the forward motion of the ball, a curveball rotates forward. The curveball spin causes the ball to drop down and move horizontally across home plate. To the batter, the pitch looks fair, and the batter swings. But the batter misses as the pitch breaks just below the bat.

There is a science to throwing a curveball. The pitcher grips the ball with his middle and index fingers together. The fingers are placed across the seams of the ball at the widest distance between the seams. Keeping a tight grip on the ball, the pitcher turns his or her wrist and snaps it down as he or she releases it. The spin that results causes the ball to slow down when it encounters resistance from the wind. From the point of view of the batter, this ball looks like it will do one thing, and then it does something different.

Answer the questions about the reading.

1. The word *banned* in paragraph 2 means ____.
   a. having put a banner across something
   b. allowed something to continue
   c. forbade someone from doing something
   d. saying one thing and doing another

2. Why is the pitch described in this reading called a curveball? _____

3. Which is faster, a fastball or a curveball? _____ Circle the sentence in the story that is a clue.

4. According to the reading, a spin that goes in reverse of the forward motion of the ball is called a _____.

5. The author's purpose in writing this passage is to ____.
   a. entertain
   b. persuade
   c. share an opinion
   d. inform

6. Sandy Koufax was called the "man with the golden arm." What do you think that means?
   _____

7. If you wanted more information about curveballs or Sandy Koufax, where could you look? Circle the correct answer or answers.
   a. in the library
   b. in an encyclopedia
   c. in a baseball reference book
   d. in a dictionary
   e. on the Internet

8. When does a pitcher put the spin on a curveball? _____

9. The main idea of this reading is ____
   a. Curveballs are good pitches to learn.
   b. Curveball are effective pitches that are easy to learn to throw.
   c. Curveballs frustrate batters.
   d. Sandy Koufax was a great pitcher.

10. A curveball rotates forward. *True* or *false*? _____

From Sketch to Sky

The Thanksgiving Day Parade hosted by Macy's in New York City is one of the most anticipated events of the holiday season. Every year, thousands of people gather to catch sight of the parade's giant, helium-filled balloons.

In 1928, four years after the very first Macy's Thanksgiving Day Parade, these large balloons were first included in the festivities. The colorful creations were used in the parade and then allowed to float around the city for days. Address labels attached to the balloons gave anyone who found the wayward giants a chance to collect a prize for returning them to Macy's.

As the parade grew, so did the collection of balloon characters. In 1934, the famous Mickey Mouse balloon joined the parade. Did you know that a rainstorm during the 1957 parade filled Popeye's cap with water and the giant balloon swerved off course, spilling water on sidewalks and spectators? Within a few years, Superman, Snoopy, and Kermit the Frog joined the ranks, along with Underdog and Bullwinkle. Most recent additions include Garfield, Elmo, and Spongebob Squarepants.

How do these giant balloons make their way from an idea on someone's sketch pad to the streets of New York City? After a two-dimensional drawing of the character is completed, it is approved by engineers. They need to make sure the design will work as a balloon. The next step is to create a clay model of the balloon. The model is built to scale, which means that it includes every detail, only smaller. Then a second model is created. This one is painted with the precise colors and details that will be duplicated on the balloon. Balloon makers are now ready to make pattern pieces of the creation.

After patterns are cut out of polyurethane, the strong, synthetic material used to make the floating balloons, the final shape is formed. Each balloon is made of separate chambers and feature large zippers, inflation devices, and a high-pressure valve. Now it is time to assemble all the pieces. The team of balloon technicians fills the balloon with helium and takes it for a test run. They inflate all of the balloon's chambers to make sure they won't leak. This is generally done at a football stadium, where there is plenty of room to maneuver and ensure that the balloon is safe and ready for the big day.

Then, on the night before Thanksgiving, the balloon and all the others to appear in the parade are inflated. Rain or shine, these balloons are anchored and marched along the parade route with the help of hundreds of volunteers.

Answer the questions about the reading.

1. In what year did the first large helium-filled balloon appear in the Macy's Thanksgiving Day Parade? _____

1924   1928   1932   1957

2. This story is an example of nonfiction. How do you know that?

_____

3. When something is *anticipated*, it means that it is _____.
   a. looked forward to   **b.** dreaded
   c. created and shown off   **d.** packed away

4. A compound word is two small words put together to make a new word. List four compound words from the reading: _____, _____, _____, _____

5. *Scale* is a multiple-meaning word. Which of the definitions below matches the way *scale* is used in the reading? _____
   a. a thin, flat plate that forms a snake's covering   **b.** to weigh
   c. including every detail, only smaller   **d.** to climb up and over

6. Which job on the team of balloon makers would you like to do? Why?

_____

7. What happens after the engineer approves the design for a new balloon? Underline the answer in the reading.

8. Why is it important to understand the sequence of events in a reading? _____

_____

9. The team of balloon makers inflates the balloon with helium. What does that mean? _____
   a. They let the air out of the balloon.
   b. They fill the balloon with helium so it can float.
   c. They use long ropes to anchor the balloon to the ground.
   d. They create a model and use it to form the big balloon.

10. On a separate sheet of paper, sketch your design for a new balloon. Use lots of color and predict how it will look as it floats above the crowds at the parade. Write a sentence to describe it.

Dear Editor

You are upset. At this year's parade, the balloon that you helped design and build hit a large tree branch that was sticking way out over the street. For weeks, the town board has been asking their workers to take the tree limb down. Not only is it a safety issue, but it ruined the parade: When the balloon tore, it fell to the ground and tripped members of the marching band!

Write a letter to the editor of your local newspaper that expresses how you feel. Make sure to clearly point out the reasons why a large, dead branch that is hanging out over the road should be removed. Remind town officials that many children walk to and from school along that street and that a strong wind could cause it to fall.

Dear Editor,

_____

_____

_____

_____

_____

_____

_____

_____

_____

_____

_____

And Then She Said...

Writing dialogue is not always easy. But it helps to remember that the characters in your stories should always say things that show who they truly are.

Read the story below. Then use your imagination to write dialogue, or what Jessica and Stephanie would say to each other. Make sure to put the words they say in quotation marks.

Jessica and Stephanie love going to the movies on Saturday afternoons. Jessica's mother drops them off and Stephanie's mother picks them up. The movie they saw this afternoon was about pirates. Jessica did not like the ending of the movie. Stephanie loved it. As they stood outside the theater and waited for their ride home, Jessica began to tell her friend why she didn't like the ending.

"I thought the ending was too sad," said Jessica.

_____

_____

_____

_____

_____

_____

_____

_____

_____

Word by Word

If you were an editor for the Merriam-Webster Dictionary, you might often be asked how you choose the new words that are included in the dictionary's next edition. According to the reference book company's website, the answer is simple. The decision's all about how a word is used and how often it is used.

Every day, many of the Merriam-Webster editors spend more than an hour reading as much as they can. They read newspapers, books, magazines, and published work on the Internet. As they read, they look for new words, how they are spelled, and how they are used. Then the editors mark or make note of each word they find, along with the other words around it. Keeping the word in context is important to the editors. After they are finished reading for the day, the editors then record their findings in a computer, where the words are stored and printed on small pieces of paper called citations.

When choosing new words to include in their dictionary, Merriam-Webster editors need to have as much information as possible. That's why, along with the word itself, a citation must include other important data, such as an example of how the word is used in context and where the word was found. Editors began using this citation system in the 1880s and now there are almost 16 million examples of words and their context clues in the dictionary database. But having an entry in the citation file does not guarantee that a new word enters the dictionary.

The next step in the process is called a review. Definers, or editors who decide whether entries already in the dictionary stay, go, or need to be updated and revised, look over citations to determine whether or not a word will be awarded its own entry. The more citations a word has, the better chance it has of making the cut. The word must also have been used in a variety of places during a significant amount of time. Another factor that affects the decision is the size of the dictionary. The smaller the dictionary is, the fewer new words that can be added. The ones that are added must be the most commonly used words.

It is a big responsibility for Merriam-Webster editors. Words appearing in their dictionaries reflect the way people live and the words they are using. So the next time you flip through your dictionary, think of the editors who decide which words stay and which ones go.

Answer the questions about the reading.

1. The two most important factors editors use to decide which new words to include in their dictionary are _____ and _____.
   a. how long the word is
   b. how the word is used
   c. how the word is spelled
   d. how often the word is used

2. The first thing editors do to choose new words for the dictionary is _____
   _____

3. Context clues are important as you read. Using context clues, write the meaning of the word *data*. _____

4. A *citation* is _____.
   a. a handwritten clue
   b. a ticket
   c. information printed on small pieces of paper
   d. a computer program that stores important information

5. If an editor collected 20 citations a week, how many citations would that editor have by the end of the year? _____

6. The more _____ a word has, the better chance it has in being included in the dictionary's next edition.

7. Choosing words for the dictionary is a big responsibility because _____.
   a. lots of people read the dictionary to find new words
   b. the dictionary reflects the way people live and words they are using
   c. they get paid well and want to do a good job
   d. editors want to make sure everyone knows the meanings of all words

8. Underline the sentence in the reading that helped you answer question 7.

9. If you were one of the editors, how would you decide what words should be included in the dictionary?_____

10. Find a word in the dictionary that you don't know and learn what it means. Use it in a sentence here. _____
   _____

Pet Rocks and Pez

From goldfish-swallowing to hula hoop–twirling, fads have come and gone throughout the years. Some fads your parents and grandparents remember. There might even be a crazy fad happening right now. Maybe someday you will even start your own.

A fad is any temporary thing, idea, or way of doing something that is taken up by a group of people. It can be anything relating to sports, fashion, or culture, but it always has to be followed in an enthusiastic way.

Take the pet rock, for example. In 1975, a salesman named Gary Dahl, of California, was joking around with some friends about how easy his pet was to take care of. He was talking about a rock. He told his friends that his pet didn't have to be fed, and it was very quiet and well behaved. It never chewed up his furniture or barked at his neighbors. As a result, Mr. Dahl began selling the Pet Rock. It came with a funny manual that instructed pet rock owners on how to handle their new pet. It even listed tricks to teach the rock. The Pet Rock fad made Mr. Dahl a millionaire. In 1976, it was the biggest fad in America. This fad lasted only a few years. But that's the way with fads. Some last months, and some are around for a year or two.

Then there's Pez. Invented in 1927, Pez started out as little candy mints sold in a small tin. Twenty years later, the candies were marketed in dispensers with cartoon heads. Pez and Pez dispensers caught on in the 1950s and have been a popular fad since.

One of the biggest fads of all time, however, is the hula hoop. Wham-O, the company that manufactured hula hoops, sold 25 million of them in the two months after they were introduced in 1957. This fad lasted more than 20 years, and hula hoops are still sold today. Other popular fads at that time were ant farms, poodle skirts, and Frisbees.

Throughout history, fads have arrived and passed. In the 1980s, Cabbage Patch Kids and the Teenage Mutant Ninja Turtles were popular toys. Then, in the 1990s, Americans were so crazy about Furby, the first interactive fuzzy toy, that it was hard to find them in stores. At the turn of the century, MySpace, camera phones, and MP3 players came on the scene.

Fads come and go, but one thing is certain: there will always be a fad or two for every generation to go crazy over.

Answer the questions about the reading.

1. The author's purpose in writing this passage is to _____.

    a. tell about a special time in his or her life   **b.** entertain readers

    c. persuade readers to think a certain way   **d.** inform or teach readers something new

2. If something is temporary, that means it is brief or passing. *True* or *false*? _____

3. Circle all the words in the word bank that help describe what a fad is.

temporary   fun   permanent   unpopular   enthusiasm

4. When was Pez invented? _____

5. What conclusion can you draw about Gary Dahl, the inventor of the Pet Rock?

_____

6. Circle key phrases in the reading that helped you draw a conclusion about Gary Dahl.

7. Why do you think fads are temporary? _____

_____

8. Other than hula hoops, name two fads during the 1950s. _____

_____

9. The word *manufactured* in paragraph 5 means _____.

    a. sold   **b.** produced

    c. talked about   **d.** taken off the market

10. Can you think of a fad you might be enjoying right now? Write a sentence that describes it.

_____

_____

Under the Sea

Have you ever wondered what really goes on under the sea? Have you ever pondered the number of sea creatures that thrive miles below the surface of the ocean's wavy water? Do you think that scientists can really find ways to warn people about earthquakes and series of waves called tsunamis? Well, a geophysicist named Marcus Gerhardt Langseth wondered those same things.

Langseth was working at the Earth Institute at Columbia University when he began studying computed axial tomography, or CAT scans. He wondered if the same scans and images used by doctors to diagnose disease in humans could be used to examine the ocean floor. He decided that the same technology could be applied to uncover the ocean's secrets.

An expert on what goes on under the sea, Langseth invented a research ship that would help scientists learn more about the oceans. He drew plans and worked with the U.S. National Science Foundation to create the *R/V Marcus G. Langseth*, or the *Langseth*, for short.

The *Langseth* began as a big ship used by geologists to search the earth's seas for oil. The National Science Foundation bought the ship for more than $20 million. The organization hired scientists and builders to spend months transforming the large vessel into a floating laboratory.

The *Langseth* is 235 feet long and weighs 2,578 tons. It houses multibeam sonar equipment which can accurately chart deep-sea floors. It carries sensitive instruments that are used to monitor earthquakes and detect waves, tides, and tsunamis. The *Langseth* also has special equipment that can record long-distance sounds and calls made by marine mammals.

First, the *Langseth* sends pulses in the form of sound waves to the sea floor. As the pulses return to the surface of the water, scientists use hydrophones, or special instruments used to detect and monitor sound under water, to read them. These three-dimensional images enable scientists to study the bottom of the ocean, including documenting faults on the sea floor, charting the topography, or features, of the ocean's bottom, and investigating marine mammals. The images and data captured by the *Langseth* are better and clearer than images produced by any other research ship. These impressive images, together with sophisticated computer equipment and technology, give scientists more information than they have ever had before.

Humans make a lot of noise, too. Biologists are concerned that underwater sounds made by people, such as engine noises from boats, disturb the lives of sea creatures. The *Langseth* plans to steer clear of marine mammals while it does its job. That way, the scientists' work will truly benefit both humans and animals.

Answer the questions about the reading.

1. Name one reason why Marcus Langseth invented the *R/V Marcus G. Langseth*.

_____

2. Which phrase defines the word *tsunami*? _____

    a. a fish stew
        b. a series of waves in the sea

    c. a large fishing ship
      d. instruments used to hear sound waves

3. Describe a job you might like to do on the *R/V Marcus G. Langseth*.

_____

4. It is important for scientists to predict tsunamis and earthquakes so they can warn people before a natural disaster strikes. *True* or *false*? _____

5. *Hydro-* means water; *-phon* means sound; and *geo-* means earth. What do you think the following words mean?

hydrophone _____

geophysicist _____

6. Use the words from the word bank to complete the sentences.

Scientists send _____ down to the ocean floor.

The _____ return to the surface. Then scientists use a

_____ to monitor the data.

             hydrophone   sound waves   pulses

7. Why are scientists concerned with how noisy humans are? _____

_____

8. Do you think the *Langseth* could be used for other purposes? Predict other ways scientists can use the *Langseth* _____

_____.

9. How do CAT scans used by doctors and the sound waves used by scientists on the *Langseth* differ? _____

_____

10. Scientists plan to steer clear of marine mammals because _____.

    a. they don't want to learn about them

    b. they believe that the sea animals may try to attack them

    c. they are concerned with how the sound made by the ship may affect sea creatures

    d. they believe it is the marine biologists' job to study underwater life

Water, Water Everywhere

We take them to ballgames, carry them in our backpacks, and grab ones to go when we leave the house. Bottled water has become big business. But how did this hydration craze get started?

The health benefits of drinking water have been known for thousands of years. When the Romans built their empire, they made sure there were plenty of sources of clean water to drink. Great leaders and famous generals sought clean, fresh water for their men and horses.

Two-thirds of our bodies consist of water. An average-sized adult can survive for up to two months without food, but would die in a few days without water. Water is very important to our health. It helps keep our bodies working properly by aiding digestion and the absorption of food. It removes toxins, or poisons, from the body, and it protects tissues and organs such as the heart, lungs, brain, and spinal cord. Water helps carry oxygen throughout the body by way of the bloodstream, and it regulates body temperature. When you don't drink enough water, you can get dehydrated.

Dehydration is a serious problem. If left untreated, it can lead to high blood pressure, allergies, headaches, and asthma. Feeling thirsty is one of the first signs of dehydration. Many health experts advise adults to drink 8 to 10 full glasses of water every day. Bottled water is a convenient way for many to do that.

Water was first bottled in the 1850s in France. At about the same time, Poland Spring, a natural spring water company in Maine, began selling three-gallon jugs of spring water. In the early years of this new industry, only the wealthy and privileged enjoyed drinking water from the glass or stoneware bottles it was sold in. As bottling methods changed and more and more people demanded bottled water, it became available to everyone.

In 1968, Vittel, a water bottling company in France, introduced the first plastic bottles. Twenty years later, companies began using a newly invented plastic material that was recyclable. This new material was lighter and stronger and revolutionized the industry.

At that point, bottled water was portable. As more and more people became aware of the importance of drinking water, the water-bottling companies grew and their products changed. For example, Poland Spring recently introduced the lightest half-liter bottle ever. Designed to be held and carried more easily, it is made with less material. According to the Poland Spring Web site, the new bottles are made with 30 percent less plastic. That's good for the environment. Even better for the earth is to drink from a faucet or fountain, but drink water wherever you can. Your body needs it!

Answer the questions about the reading.

1. Why has bottled water become so popular?

_____

2. Underline the statement below that is **not** a benefit of drinking lots of water.

   It helps our bodies digest food.

   It removes toxins and protects tissues.

   It helps carry oxygen throughout the body.

   It makes our bodies slow down and sweat less.

3. When people don't drink enough water, they can become _____.

4. Doctors recommend that adults drink _____ glasses of water each day.

   a. 4 to 6   **b.** 8 to 10   **c.** 2 to 3   **d.** 12 to 14

5. What inference can you make about why only wealthy people could enjoy bottled water during the 1850s?

_____

6. Plastic water bottles made drinking water portable. That means that the plastic bottles were _____.

   a. heavier

   b. taller and harder to hold

   c. lighter and stronger

   d. the same as the glass ones

7. Poland Spring introduced a newly designed plastic bottle made from _____ percent less plastic.

8. Poland Spring's new plastic bottles were lightweight but more difficult to carry around. *True* or *false*? _____

9. The main idea of this reading is that _____

_____.

10. Imagine a new plastic bottle for drinking water. Think about portability and weight. Explain two changes you would make to today's bottle.

_____

_____

How Does a Spud Get Out of the Ground?

Something happens in northern Maine every fall. As the leaves change color and the air begins to chill, farmers dust off large machinery and get ready to pull the state's potato crop out of the ground. One of America's top potato-producing states, Maine has the perfect climate for growing tubers. Maine's potato industry is big business. It employs more than 6,100 people and brings money back into the state each year.

From French fries to potato chips to baked potatoes, the Maine potato comes in many varieties. For example, red potatoes and Ontario and Superior varieties are popular tablestock. That means they are suited to be eaten boiled, baked, or mashed. Maine farmers also grow seed potatoes. These are the ones used by farmers to plant the next season's crop of taters. Seed potatoes are usually less than two inches long. They are planted two to four inches deep and ten to eighteen inches apart. Most potato varieties take from 90 to 100 days to mature, or become adult plants ready for harvest.

Farmers spray their crops with a special herbicide that kills the plants' tops, or the green, leafy part that grows above the ground. Once the tops turn brown, schools close and many students begin working in the harvest. Young people who work do not miss any school. The schools close in mid-September for four to five weeks and reopen in October.

Years ago, elementary school children participated in the potato harvest by working on hand crews. They woke up early in the morning and dressed in sweatshirts, jeans, and work boots. Carrying work gloves and a big lunch, the children headed to the fields to pick up potatoes after the farmer plowed them out of the ground. The farmer paid the children for every barrel they filled with potatoes.

Older students still work on potato harvesters, which are large equipment pulled by tractors. The harvester digs the potatoes and carries them onto the machinery by a long, moving belt. Working on a harvester requires picking rocks and rotten potatoes off the belt as the spuds bounce by. The potatoes then move up another belt and are dumped into a truck that rides alongside.

Call them spuds, tubers, or taters, those Maine potatoes need everyone's help to get out of the ground.

Answer the questions about the reading.

1. Name three uses for the Maine potato: _____, _____, and _____.

2. Two reasons why Maine's potato industry is good for the state are that _____ and _____.
   a. it employs more than 6,100 people   **b.** it gets more people to come visit the state
   c. it gives teachers time off during the fall   **d.** it brings money back into the state

3. In this reading, the potato is referred to by three other names: _____, _____, and _____.

4. The author wrote this passage to inform readers about the Maine potato harvest. Circle two things you learned.

5. Putting events in the correct order is important to understanding a story. Which of the following events are described in the correct order, according to the reading? _____
   a. The harvester digs the potatoes out of the ground and students transport them out of the fields.
   b. The potatoes die and then farmers use a plow to pull them out of the ground before packing them for shipment.
   c. Farmers kill the potato tops and then dig them out of the ground.
   d. Trucks wait in the fields as children put potatoes into barrels and then dump them in.

6. Do you think that working on a harvester would be a hard job? Why or why not?
   _____

7. If a farmer paid you $2.25 for every barrel you filled with potatoes and you filled 11 by the end of the day, how much money would you earn? _____

8. How long does it take for a seed potato to grow into an adult potato plant?
   _____

9. Farmers know that it's time to harvest potatoes when _____.
   a. they pull a few up and check
   b. they see that the potato tops are brown and dead
   c. the calendar says that 100 days have passed
   d. their neighbors start digging their potatoes

Potato Pancakes

Maine's northernmost county is Aroostook County. The people who live there have learned to cook many different dishes with their native crop: potatoes. They make potato candy, called Needhams. They also make stews, soups, pancakes, and cakes that all use mashed or cooked potatoes.

Think of your favorite food. Make up a new recipe for it, but include potatoes as one of the ingredients. Use the outline below to help you write the recipe. Remember to consider how some foods go together, and some foods don't.

Be creative. That's how many famous chefs got started!

Recipe title: _____

Ingredients:

_____

_____

_____

_____

_____

Directions:

_____

_____

_____

_____

_____

_____

_____

This or That?

When Nick and Kristina are bored, they play a made-up game called This or That. In the game, each asks the other a question that gives a choice to do this or that. For example, would you rather eat pizza or ice cream? Then they write down each other's answers and make up a short story. Sometimes they illustrate their stories or make them into cartoon strips. The important thing about This or That is to try to learn as much about the other person as you can.

Think about your brother, sister, or friend. Make a list of This or That questions that you want to ask him or her. Have them do the same for you. Then ask away. When you are finished, you will have probably learned something interesting about the other person. Nick and Kristina always do!

Below are a few sample questions for you to practice with. Write your answers on the lines. Ready, set, go. Which would you rather do…this or that?

1. Would you rather go to the beach or go snowboarding? _____

2. Would you rather wear boots on a rainy day or splash through puddles in bare feet?

_____

3. Would you rather watch the news or watch cartoons? _____

4. Would you rather take a long walk or take a long nap? _____

5. Would you rather sing a song in front of a room filled with people or sing in the shower?

_____

6. Would you rather be the lead in a play or work on scenery? _____

7. Would you rather ride on a rollercoaster or a merry-go-round? _____

8. Would you rather do your homework as soon as you get home or wait until after dinner?

_____

9. Would you rather rake leaves or shovel snow? _____

Keys to an Awesome Summer

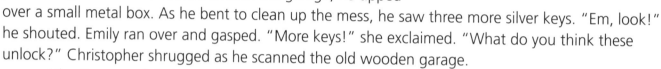

Emily and Christopher had no idea what the small, rusty key belonged to. They found it when they were helping their mother create a flowerbed in their backyard. After three weeks of an unbearably boring summer vacation, the dull clink of Emily's shovel as it hit the silver key promised an adventure.

"Maybe it belonged to a pirate," said Christopher as they carried the key inside to wash it off.

"Or a rich young girl who hid a treasure somewhere here in town," Emily added excitedly as she carefully dropped the key into her jewelry box.

Later, as Christopher quickly pulled his bicycle from its position against the old work bench in the garage, he tipped over a small metal box. As he bent to clean up the mess, he saw three more silver keys. "Em, look!" he shouted. Emily ran over and gasped. "More keys!" she exclaimed. "What do you think these unlock?" Christopher shrugged as he scanned the old wooden garage.

Like the rest of their new home, the garage was built in the early 1900s. It stood beside the house at the end of a long, dirt driveway. Emily knew what her brother was thinking, and they both started walking slowly inside the garage. Emily stopped at one of the narrow windows when she spotted something resting in the corner of one of the panes. She reached up and found a small brown envelope. Carefully, she unpeeled the discolored flap and found two more keys.

"Look," she motioned to Christopher just as he lunged toward a brownish glass bottle that had been jammed between two wooden boards in the floor. There was a clinking sound as he pried the bottle free. He tipped the bottle and six more keys slid into his hand along with lots of sawdust and dead bugs. Emily wrinkled her nose in disgust.

The two continued their search. They spent hours hunting for more keys. They scoured the large cellar and found fourteen more keys. They crawled around the dusty attic and found eleven more. Emily checked her closet and the kitchen, while Christopher checked the rest of the rooms. Together they found nine more keys.

Later that day, Emily and Christopher rode their bikes to town hall to find a list of their home's former residents. They learned that a minister and his family were the home's first occupants. A doctor and a politican had also lived there. As Christopher moved his finger down the document, Emily's eyes grew wide. "Look," she said. As Christopher read the entry before theirs, they started to laugh.

"We thought the keys would lead us to a treasure," said Christopher. "Instead, the keys belonged to a…

"Locksmith!" they said together.

When Christopher and Emily returned home, they cleaned off the keys and made a large wind chime. They hung the chime on their front porch—a tribute to all the new possibilities and unopened doors that awaited them in their new home.

Answer the questions about the story.

1. Circle the clues in the story that tell you that Emily and Christopher had just moved into a new house.

2. How many keys did Christopher and Emily find altogether? _____

3. The author's purpose in writing this story is to ____.

    a. inform   **b.** share an opinion

    c. teach about a time in history   **d.** entertain

4. Have you ever found anything interesting? Write a sentence describing what you found.

_____

_____

5. After reading this story, I think that a *locksmith* is ____.

    a. a person who unlocks mysteries   **b.** a person who makes or repairs locks and keys

    c. a person who builds doors and windows   **d.** a person who likes to read about houses

6. Adverbs are words that describe actions. Many of them end with *–ly*. List some adverbs from the story.

_____

7. Write a sentence that describes what you think Emily and Christopher might do next.

_____

_____

8. What are some reasons why you think Emily and Christopher were bored?

_____

_____

9. When Emily sees _____, she wrinkles her nose.

10. Christopher found the first key. *True* or *false*? _____

A Fun Dining Experience

Not many original diners are still around today. But if you are lucky enough to find one, going inside will feel like going back in time.

A diner is a prefabricated restaurant. That means it is built in parts or sections in one place before it is delivered and assembled in another. Historically found throughout parts of New York and New Jersey, diners serve a wide range of American food. Authentic diners are famous for their casual and relaxed atmosphere, and a long counter and booths where customers sit and eat. They are generally open all day and night.

The first diner was a lunch wagon that served hot food to the people who worked at the *Providence Journal*, a newspaper in Providence, Rhode Island. This horse-drawn wagon was owned by a man named Walter Scott, who used the wagon to supplement, or add to, the income he made at his regular job. This was in 1872. By the end of the 1800s, lunch wagons that could seat customers began being manufactured and popped up in busy cities in the northeastern United States. By 1925, the term *lunch wagon* was replaced by *diner*.

People who wanted to start their own restaurant business, but couldn't afford it, discovered that setting up a diner was a profitable alternative. Throughout the 1950s, diners became attractive small business opportunities. Even in the 1970s, when fast-food restaurants began to spring up everywhere, diners remained a big part of life in New York and New Jersey.

The first diners were narrow and long. They resembled dining cars on trains. The service counter, including floor-mounted stools for customers, took up a large amount of space in original diners. Larger ones may have had a row of booths lined up along the front wall. Many diners of the 1950s had stainless steel panels, glass blocks, and neon signs. One of the most well-known features of a diner, however, was its grill.

Much of the food served at diners was grilled. Cooks made hamburgers, French fries, club sandwiches, fried eggs, hot dogs, and pancakes. Pie was the typical dessert. Diners also had a unique language for the food they served. In the first diners, waitresses used shorthand, or a shortened language, when placing an order for food. For example, if a waitress asked the cook to make a "stack of Vermont," it meant she was ordering a stack of pancakes with maple syrup. An "all-hot" was a baked potato and a "radio" was a tuna salad sandwich on toast.

Stepping into a real diner is like stepping into America in the 1950s. The food may have changed somewhat, but the feeling will most likely still be there.

Complete the retelling of the reading.

A building that is made in one place and delivered and assembled in another is called a
1. _____ structure. That is how diners were set up. A casual place to grab
dinner, diners are famous for their 2. _____, _____,
and _____.

The first diner was a lunch wagon pulled by a 3. _____. By 1925,
however, people began calling them 4. _____. Here's what diners looked
like inside:
5. _____ .

Most of the food was grilled at diners. The menu consisted of foods such as
6. _____, _____, _____,
and _____. Waitresses used a shortened language to place orders. For
example, an "all-hot" was a baked potato.

7. Congratulations. You now know a lot about diners. Now create your own menu. Just fill in
the blanks. Don't forget to name your diner and make up shorthand words for your dishes, so that
the waitresses know how to place their orders.

_____ Diner

Pancakes   .... $1.99   .... stack of Vermont

_____......................_____......................_____

_____......................_____......................_____

_____......................_____......................_____

_____......................_____......................_____

Yawn, It's Contagious!

What is the first thing you want to do when you see someone yawn? You want to yawn, too! It's no secret that yawning is contagious, but why do we yawn at all?

Before we get to that, grab a pencil and a piece of paper. Keep track of how many times you yawn while you read this. Just reading and thinking about yawning often makes us yawn.

Back to the reason. Well, scientists are not really sure why we yawn. They do know, however, that all people yawn. They also know that some reptiles, birds, and most mammals yawn. But because there is very little research about yawning, it's not clear exactly why we do it.

Most people yawn when they are bored or tired. The average yawn lasts about six seconds. Babies start to yawn even before they are born. The earliest yawn takes place when a baby is still inside its mother. When young children are about one year old, they start to yawn when they see others yawning. That's why scientists seem to think yawning is contagious.

Boredom does have something to do with yawning. In a recent study, scientists observed students between the ages of 17 and 19. They compared the number of yawns they saw in students watching music videos to students watching a boring, color test pattern. The study found that the young people who watched the test pattern yawned more times and their yawns lasted longer than the students who were watching videos.

Another theory about yawning and boredom has to do with breathing. Some experts believe that when we are bored or tired, we breathe more slowly. As our breathing slows down, we are not getting rid of as much carbon dioxide in our bodies. These experts believe it begins to build up and sends a signal to the brain to breathe deeply. The result is a big yawn. This theory, however, was proven incorrect in 1987.

In 2007, researchers proposed a new theory. They suggested that the reason people yawn is to cool down their brains. These scientists found that people who were warmer than others yawn more frequently.

Scientists are still trying to figure out why yawning occurs and why it is so contagious. But one thing they know for sure is true is that when one person yawns, just about everyone else nearby wants to yawn, too!

Answer the questions about the reading.

1. How many times did you yawn while you were reading this? _____

2. The main idea of this reading is that _____.
    a. scientists aren't sure why we yawn, but they are sure it is contagious
    b. animals and birds yawn more than people
    c. people yawn to get more oxygen in their bodies and cool down their brains
    d. yawning puts most people to sleep

3. The average yawn lasts about _____ seconds.

4. Describe your favorite theory about yawning from the reading.
_____
_____

5. The word *proposed* in paragraph 7 means the same as _____.
    yawned   suggested   covered up   studied

6. Write the definition for the word *contagious*.
_____
_____

7. How do you think scientists know that animals and birds yawn?
_____
_____

8. Underline the sentence that is **not** a theory about yawning.
    People yawn because they are bored.
    People yawn to get more oxygen and release carbon dioxide.
    People yawn for attention.
    People yawn when they see other people yawn.

9. Why do you think you yawn? Explain your theory.
_____
_____

10. Reread pg. 38 and record how many times you yawn while reading it. Compare the reading results to your first count from question 1. Why do you think the counts differ in that way?
_____

Palindrome Party

Palindromes are words that are spelled the same in both directions. For example, the word *pop* is spelled the same forward and backward. So is the word *mom*. See if you can list more examples of words that are palindromes.

_____

_____

_____

Palindromes can also be whole sentences. For example, the sentence *Del saw a sled* uses the same sequence of letters when you read the sentence forward and backward. Even though the letters aren't spaced correctly when you write the sentence backwards, it uses the same letters. Try writing it backward!

Del saw a sled. _____

Now look at this box of words, phrases, and sentences. Circle the ones that are palindromes.

Step on no pets.	Was it a car or a cat I saw?
Was it a cat I saw?	Nurses run.
Ma has a ham.	noon
Go play in the yard.	racecar
level	A fish swims in a lake.
pencil	kayak

Details, Details

Sometimes we are in such a hurry that we don't notice details of the things we see. Think about something you did recently. Can you describe what one of your companions was wearing? Can you remember the colors or the clothing and exactly the things you saw? Would you be able to describe everything in detail to a friend?

Look around and pick one thing that you see right now. Spend a few minutes looking at it. Try to find ways to remember what you are seeing. Examine and study its color and texture, what the object or person is doing, how it moves, if it makes noises, or if it is moving or standing still.

Now turn away from the object you chose and write for one minute without stopping. Write down everything you remember about it.

_____

_____

_____

_____

_____

_____

Read what you wrote and look at the object again. Did you remember everything that was important about the object you chose? If you could add one more detail, what would it be?

_____

Icy, Cold, and Beautiful

It is cold and dark outside. You are looking up into the night sky. What you see is bright and colorful and changing. Described as fingers of light, the aurora borealis you are admiring are caused by a complex series of events that originates at the sun.

Aurora borealis, more commonly known as the Northern Lights, can usually be seen in the northern part of the United States. They are colored light displays that sometimes look like a greenish glow. The lights are named for Aurora, the Roman goddess of the dawn, and Boreas, the Greek god of the north wind. Aurora borealis are only visible in the northern hemisphere, or the half of Earth between the equator and the North Pole. The best chances to see this phenomenon are from September to October and March to April.

Aurora borealis are formed when large amounts of solar particles are thrown off during big explosions and flares on the sun's surface. These particles are propelled deep into space. They travel in clouds at a very high speed. Sometimes it takes two to three days for one of these particle clouds to reach Earth. But when it does, it is captured by the magnetosphere, or earth's magnetic field, which guides the cloud toward the North Pole.

As the particles head toward earth, they are blocked by the atmosphere. Our atmosphere is like a gaseous envelope surrounding the earth. It is like a force field or shield around our planet. So, when the particles try to get close, they crash into the gases that are floating around in the atmosphere. These collisions between the solar particles and the gas particles cause lights that appear to move across the sky. These collisions cause the Northern Lights.

Knowing what they are and having the opportunity to actually see aurora borealis is tricky. For many people, seeing these shimmering fingers of light is more about luck than timing. According to astronomers, however, location is the key factor.

Most auroral displays happen on an oval-shaped area that looks like a donut above the North Pole. This imaginary donut changes its position as it rotates with the sun. It also can change in size, growing bigger and smaller in a short amount of time. Because of these factors, it can be difficult to predict exactly when aurora borealis will be out and lighting up the sky.

Patience is key. If you wait long enough and keep looking up in the north sky, your chances of viewing the Northern Lights increase. Just be sure the sky is clear. As you can imagine, clouds have a way of obstructing the gorgeous view!

Answer the questions about the reading.

1. Using context clues, what does the word *propelled* in paragraph 3 mean? ____
   a. traveled slowly away from something   **b.** moved around and changed position
   c. traveled quickly or at a high speed   **d.** remained stationary and in one place

2. I know this is an informational nonfiction article because it gives _____ about real events and things.

3. Are you more likely to see aurora borealis in Maine or Florida? _____

4. Are you more likely to see aurora borealis in the morning or at night? _____

5. What happens when the cloud of particles from the sun approach the earth? ____
   a. They break up and go away.   **b.** They collide with particles in earth's atmosphere.
   c. They race toward the oceans on earth.   **d.** They float around in the atmosphere.

6. The author gives some advice about where to see the Northern Lights. Circle the sentences in the reading that give that information.

7. The best times to see aurora borealis are during the months of ____ and ____.
   a. May and June   **b.** September and October
   c. January and February   **d.** March and April

8. What other advice does the author give us about seeing aurora borealis?
   _____

   _____

9. The earth's magnetic field is called the _____.

10. The author wrote this passage to ____.
   a. entertain   **b.** tell about an event in his or her life
   c. inform or teach something new   **d.** persuade

Live Strong Like Lance

Lance Armstrong was ranked the seventh fastest cyclist in the world when he was diagnosed with cancer. Given less than a 50-50 chance of surviving the devastating disease, Lance employed the same determination he used to win races to beat cancer. Because of his strong will and good attitude, Lance later won both bicycle races and life.

Born on September 18, 1971, in Plano, Texas, Lance was raised in Dallas by his mother. An athlete at a young age, he began running and swimming when he was 10 years old. He began competing in cycling races and triathlons, which are races that combine running, swimming, and cycling, when he was 13 years old. In 1989 and 1990, Lance won two triathlon championships. He was only 16 years old. After that, Lance decided to focus his time and energy on cycling.

Lance qualified for many races and placed second in the U.S. Olympic time trials in 1992. He won three big races the following year and continued to be victorious. By the fall of 1996, Lance was one of the best cyclists in the world. He also learned that he had cancer.

By the time his doctors found the cancer, it had spread to several parts of his body, including his lungs and brain. He had surgery, changed his diet, and began chemotherapy, which is a treatment used to control and destroy cancer cells in the body. By the beginning of 1997, Lance was declared cancer-free.

Throughout his fight against cancer, Lance told everyone that he was going to compete again. It took a year for him to train and get back into shape, but he went on to win the first of seven Tour de France races. Lance's victory at the distinguished races was nothing compared to his victory over cancer. In 1996, he founded the Lance Armstrong Foundation for Cancer, or LiveStrong. He wrote two autobiographies and ran the New York City Marathon in 2006. At the race, he raised hundreds of thousands of dollars for his LiveStrong campaign.

Lance has been a successful athlete for most of his life. He has been awarded many sports honors. But it is his strength and determination in beating cancer that has made him a hero to people everywhere. Through his leadership and work on behalf of cancer survivors, Lance is a symbol of hope and an inspiration. His foundation is one of the most influential organizations, and the information and tools he passes on to people help them to work to beat cancer, too. To find out more information about Lance's organization, log on to *www.livestrong.org*.

Answer the questions about the reading.

1. When someone is given a 50-50 chance of getting better, what do you think that means?

_____

2. About how old was Lance Armstrong when he learned that he had cancer? _____

3. A triathlon is a race during which the competitors must ____.
   a. run and swim
   b. run, swim, and ride a bicycle
   c. swim, ride a bicycle, and paddle a boat
   d. ride a bicycle, run, and hit a ball

4. When did Lance decide to concentrate his efforts on only cycling? _____

5. How do you think Lance felt when the doctors told him he had cancer? _____

_____

6. Underline the sentence in the reading that supports the claim that Lance Armstrong has determination.

7. Circle the qualities in the word bank that you think Lance has.

strength   laziness   determination   poor attitude

8. How many Tour de France races has Lance won? _____

9. If you wanted more information about Lance's organization, LiveStrong, where might you find it?

_____

10. Do you think Lance is a hero? Why or why not?

_____

_____

45

Map It Out

Imagine spending your time making maps. If you were a cartographer, that's what you would be doing all the time. You might even work for the National Geospatial-Intelligence Agency.

NGA for short, the National Geospatial-Intelligence Agency is a federal agency that creates maps, charts, and images of the earth. These products are used by the U.S. Army, Navy, Air Force, Marines, and other government organizations. The products made by the NGA are also used by airplane pilots, ship captains, and anyone who needs information about the world's geography.

One of the most popular products created by cartographers at the NGA are maps. Maps are drawings of geographic places on Earth. They help people to find places, and they are used to measure distance and plan trips. Some of the maps made by cartographers are used by pilots to find airplane routes and by military planners to plan missions. Cartographers choose which features will go on a map, depending on who will be using it.

A map maker needs a lot of information beforehand. Information about roads, rivers, and buildings is collected from photographs taken from airplanes of small areas on Earth. Cartographers also use images taken by space satellites and measurements taken by the Shuttle Radar Topography Mission. During this February 2000 mission, the crew of the Space Shuttle Endeavor recorded hundreds of measurements of mountains and valleys and stored them in computer databases, or organized collections of information. The NGA has the largest collection of this type of data. The information is available to cartographers.

Once they access the necessary information, cartographers use a special software program that helps them draw maps on a computer. Years ago, before computers, map makers drew maps by hand, using pens, pencils, and paper. The process was long and expensive. A map that can be made in an hour on a computer might take a year to make by hand. That is because ensuring the information is exact is so important. A computer makes checking and rechecking information much easier. Without accurate information, a map is useless!

The next step is constructing a map legend. A map's legend lists and interprets all the symbols and colors used on the map. It also shows the map's scale, which is the difference between the actual size of the area on Earth's surface and the size it is on the map.

Today's cartographers are constantly learning new techniques and skills to make new maps. These guides need to keep up with the world as it changes.

Answer the questions about the reading.

1. What does a cartographer do?

_____

2. Write a sentence that explains how the job of a cartographer today is different from years ago.

_____

_____

3. Cartographers use information from _____ to construct maps.

   a. other maps   **b.** satellite images and photographs

   c. reference books and atlases   **d.** measurements sent in by tourists

4. Why is it so important for the information on a map to be accurate?

_____

_____

5. The purpose of a legend on a map is to _____.

   a. list and interpret the symbols and colors used on a map

   b. show how long it took to make the map

   c. persuade people to use the map

   d. show the best routes from one place to another

6. Underline the sentences in the reading that explain why cartographers make maps.

7. Look around and find a small area to make a map of. Write a sentence that describes the area.

_____

_____

8. On a separate piece of paper, sketch what you see in that area. Instead of drawing the objects themselves, place symbols on the map. For example, a small square on the map might show where a sandbox is.

9. Add a map legend to explain the symbols you used. Here is an example of a legend:

   ■ = sandbox   ▬ = swings   △ = picnic table

10. Use your map to go from one place to another. Write a sentence describing the best route.

_____

_____

Ben, Jerry, and John

John Shaffer gets to eat ice cream all day long. That is because his job title is "flavor guru" and his employers are Ben and Jerry.

Ben Cohen and Jerry Greenfield were lifelong friends. They met in the seventh grade and have been buddies ever since. In 1977, they took a correspondence course from Pennsylvania State University and learned how to make ice cream. In the following year, the two men opened their first ice cream parlor in Burlington, Vermont. During the 30 years that followed, Ben & Jerry's grew into the multi-billion-dollar ice cream company it is today. At the heart of the company's success is the creativity of people like John Shaffer, who work at the Ben & Jerry's manufacturing plant in Burlington.

Every morning, John wakes up and heads to the ice cream factory. He wasn't always a flavor guru, or expert, but John has always worked in the food industry. Once a chef, cookbook editor, and food stylist, John decided one day that he wanted to work at Ben & Jerry's. So he called them. After two years of calling and never giving up, John's persistence paid off. He was hired as a flavor inventor and spends his days concocting new flavors for Ben & Jerry's Ice Cream. Among his newest creations are Cinnamon Bun and Uncanny Cashew.

Along with inventing new flavors, John tastes ice cream every day, all day long. That may seem like a fattening job, but like the other employees at Ben & Jerry's, John is very careful not to eat too much of the cold, creamy confection. He says that the biggest perk of working there is three pints of free ice cream he and the other employees each take home every day. John says that his freezer at home is filled with different varieties of the stuff.

One of the most challenging parts of John's job is ensuring that the flavors are just right. They must be blended perfectly and taste exactly the way they are supposed to taste. If not, then he goes back to the drawing board.

About 14 months may pass as John develops an idea and tests the new flavor, and then Ben & Jerry's produces it and transports it to supermarket freezers. If the flavor is a hit, it joins the ranks of other classic flavors such as Chunky Monkey and Coconut Almond Fudge Chip. What a delicious job!

Answer the questions about the reading.

1. *Cookbook* is an example of a compound word in the reading. Find and write two more.

_____

2. Write a sentence retelling how Ben & Jerry's Ice Cream company got started.

_____

_____

3. A *guru* is _____.
   a. a winner   **b.** an expert   **c.** an ice cream maker   **d.** the owner of a company

4. Why do you think John was hired as a flavor guru?

_____

5. The author says that John is persistent. Underline the sentence in the reading that is a clue to what *persistent* means.

6. Alliteration happens when the initial sound of a word is repeated within a phrase. Write the example of alliteration found in the reading.

_____

7. Write five of your own alliterations, using your favorite flavor words to describe ice cream. For example, I love chilly chunky chocolate.

_____

_____

_____

_____

_____

8. One perk that employees at Ben & Jerry's enjoy is _____.
   a. four-day work weeks   **b.** all the chocolate they can eat
   c. free pints of ice cream   **d.** long hours

9. About _____ months may pass before a new flavor goes from just an idea to a pint in a grocery store freezer.

10. If you could invent an ice cream flavor, what would it be? What ingredients would you use?

_____

_____

Coast Guard Dogs

Dogs are said to be man's best friend. But to the U.S. Coast Guard, they are much more than that. For thousands of years, various Coast Guard crews have brought animals on their missions. Dogs have accompanied crews on voyages and assignments. Originally enlisted to catch mice aboard the ships, these animals have become more than working dogs. They have become members of the crew.

The U.S. Coast Guard is one of the seven military branches in America. The role of the Coast Guard is to protect people, the environment, and the country in all waters, ports, and inland waterways. That means they enforce the law, help boaters in trouble, and conduct search and rescue missions wherever there is water. There are more than 40,000 men and women enlisted in the Coast Guard. There are also dozens of cats and dogs.

The Coast Guard's best-known mascot is Sinbad. His title is Chief Petty Officer, Dog. Adopted in 1938 by the crew of the *Campbell*, Sinbad sailed aboard the ship during World War II. During one battle at sea, the *Campbell* was severely damaged by a German submarine. The commanding officer ordered most of the personnel off the ship, where they boarded another ship nearby. Only a few stayed on board the *Campbell* to make sure it stayed afloat as it was being towed to safety. Sinbad was one of them.

Sinbad served on board the *Campbell* for 11 years. He was made a member of the crew and had all the official forms, paperwork, and uniforms. He even had his own bunk on the ship, just like the other crew members. Sinbad retired from the Coast Guard and lived the rest of his life at the Barnegat Light Station in New Jersey.

Sinbad is only one of the many mascots adopted by crews to keep them company at sea. Bear, who retired from 10 years of Coast Guard service in 2000, served at the station in Kenosha, Wisconsin. A purebred chocolate Labrador retriever, Bear came to be a member of the Coast Guard as a puppy. He loved to ride on the boats, especially on the back of the crew's jet ski. He patrolled the beaches during storms, accompanied sailors on their missions, and entertained schoolchildren who visited the station on field trips. Like Sinbad, the crew at Kenosha was sad to see Bear retire.

For more information about Coast Guard animals, just go to the U.S. Coast Guard's website.

Answer the questions about the reading.

1. Although the reading doesn't define the word *mascot*, you can use context clues to figure out that a mascot is _____.
   a. any kind of animal
   b. people who adopt animals to help them
   c. an animal adopted by a group to represent them
   d. a sailor or person who travels

2. Place a check next to the sentences that describe what the U.S. Coast Guard does.
   a. _____ enforces laws
   b. _____ helps boaters in trouble
   c. _____ conducts search and rescue missions at sea
   d. _____ keeps traffic running smoothly on roads and highways

3. What qualities do you think are important for Coast Guard mascots to have?

_____

4. The Coast Guard's best-known mascot is _____ .

5. Bear worked for the Coast Guard for _____ years.

6. The word *personnel* in paragraph 3 means _____.
   a. the people or staff who work for an organization
   b. food and clothing
   c. guests who are onboard the ship
   d. the mascot

7. What do you think these sentences imply about the relationship between the dogs and the sailors: *Originally enlisted to catch mice aboard the ships, these animals have become more than working dogs. They have become members of the crew.*

_____

8. On ships, bunks are where the sailors _____.
   a. eat   **b.** go to play   **c.** sleep   **d.** work

9. Which do you think would make a better Coast Guard mascot, a dog or a cat? Explain why.

_____

_____

10. How can you find more information about Coast Guard mascots?

_____

My Life as a Dog

An interview is a great way to learn more about a person who interests you, especially if you would like to write a story or need to write a report. By interviewing, you get answers to your questions.

On the previous pages you read about Coast Guard mascots. These are brave dogs that sail with men and women who serve their country. Imagine that you could talk to a Coast Guard dog and ask it anything at all. What would you ask? More importantly, how do you think the dog would respond?

Below is a typical interview format. First fill in the questions you would like to ask the Coast Guard dog. The Q next to the blank lines stands for "Questions." Then go back and pretend to be the dog. Answer the questions. Write the answers on the appropriate lines marked A.

My Life as a Coast Guard Dog

Q: _____

A: _____

Q: _____

A: _____

Q: _____

A: _____

Q: _____

A: _____

Q: _____

A: _____

Be Prepared for Anything!

    Camping can be a lot of fun. It is important, however, to make sure you bring everything you need. Think about the things you might need if you and your family or friends were to camp in a tent for two nights. Think about what supplies you would need. Think about what food you would have to bring with you. Make a list below of the things you think you will need for your trip.

_____

_____

_____

_____

_____

_____

_____

_____

_____

    Lists are a good way to keep track of the things you need to do or bring on a trip. The next time you are planning to go somewhere, write a short list to make sure you don't forget anything important!

Everyone Loves Eleanor

In a story published in *Look Magazine* in 1951, Eleanor Roosevelt shared the names of seven people who inspired and influenced her life. Her heroes included her mother and father, the head teacher at the school she attended as a young girl, and her favorite aunt. In the article, however, Eleanor stated that it was her husband and her mother-in-law who most influenced the way her life developed.

Born in New York City in 1884, Eleanor Roosevelt and her brothers and sisters were raised by their grandmother after her parents died. She grew up attending a well-known and respected school in England. There she gained the self-confidence that she became known for.

In 1905, Eleanor married Franklin Delano Roosevelt. Her uncle, Theodore Roosevelt, who was the twenty-sixth president of the United States, walked her down the aisle on her wedding day. During the next 11 years, Eleanor and Franklin had six children. During that time, one of their children died and Franklin was elected to the New York State Senate. Eleanor began learning about politics by involving herself in her husband's work.

In 1921, Franklin contracted polio, a disease of the spinal cord that causes paralysis. He was brave and determined to regain the use of his legs. Eleanor stood by her husband's side and was devoted to his care. As a result, she became more involved in his political career. She helped him become elected governor of New York State seven years later. Because of Franklin's illness, Eleanor became his eyes and ears. She paid attention to the issues and concerns of the people of New York and shared everything she learned with her husband.

Franklin Delano Roosevelt was elected president in 1933 and Eleanor became First Lady. Having helped her husband throughout his political career made her both knowledgeable and graceful. She was the first wife of a president to hold press conferences, give lectures, and appear in radio broadcasts. Eleanor traveled throughout the United States and wrote a daily newspaper column called "My Day."

Eleanor Roosevelt once wrote: "No matter how plain a woman may be, if truth and loyalty are stamped upon her face, all will be attracted to her." For her, honesty and faithfulness were important rules to live by. Eleanor lived by those two rules her whole life.

When Franklin died in 1945, Eleanor went back to their cottage in Hyde Park, New York, to live. She served as spokesperson for the United Nations until she died in 1962. Eleanor is remembered most for her constant work to improve the lives of people less fortunate than she.

Answer the questions about the reading.

1. Why would *Look Magazine* write an article about Eleanor Roosevelt?

   _____

   _____

2. How did Eleanor Roosevelt learn about politics? ____
   a. by reading the newspaper   **b.** by involving herself in her husband's work
   c. by going to school   **d.** by running for the U.S. Senate

3. Write the definition of the word *polio*.

   _____

   _____

4. Why do you think Eleanor became even more involved in Franklin's work after he contracted polio?

   _____

   _____

5. Franklin Delano Roosevelt was elected president in _____.

6. Underline the words Eleanor wrote. Then use context clues to write the word that helps define the word *loyalty*: _____

7. Eleanor Roosevelt wrote a daily newspaper column. *True* or *false*? _____

8. Eleanor was the first wife of a president to do which three things? ____, ____, and ____
   a. write a book   **b.** hold press conferences
   c. give lectures   **d.** appear in radio broadcasts

9. What conclusions can you draw about the type of person Eleanor Roosevelt was?

   _____

   _____

10. How old was Eleanor Roosevelt when she died? _____

Crazy About Cupcakes

They are small. They are delicious. Everyone gets to choose exactly which one they want. It's no secret that people of all ages are crazy about cupcakes. But how did the humble cupcake get to be what it is today?

The Oxford Companion to Food defines a cupcake as any small cake baked in a cup-shaped mold or in a paper baking cup. The reference book then explains that, in America, the cupcake may have also earned its name from the cup, or the measuring system used in the baking process.

These small cakes were popular in the eighteenth century. Originally they were made from a creamy mixture that included currants, lemon zest, and chopped almonds. They were baked as individual cakes and were called Queen cakes. Queen cakes were almost like small fruitcakes, but lighter and not as dense.

There are two popular theories about the origin of the cupcake. The first one explains that the name comes from the amount of ingredients used to create the cakes. For example, cupcakes were made using one cup of flour, one cup of butter, and one cup of sugar. The other theory states that the small cakes were originally baked in small cups, like earthenware tea cups or other small clay baking pans. Either way, cupcakes were individually sized.

Today, cupcake varieties are endless. At home they can be baked in tins that can cook up to twelve little cakes at a time. They come in many different flavors and their tops can range from simple to intricate in decoration.

At the Cupcake Café in New York City, hundreds of people walk in each day to buy one or two or twelve elaborately decorated cupcakes. Known for her buttercream blossoms that sit delicately atop her cupcakes, co-owner Ann Warren uses colors, shapes, and floral arrangements as inspiration. One review of her creations stated that the flowers on top of the delicious cupcakes looked like they are blooming from roots underneath the frosting.

Stores like the Cupcake Café are baking their way throughout the United States. The popularity of the cupcake has exploded and people everywhere want to sample a taste of their childhood. Many people say that the main reason they love cupcakes as adults is because it reminds them of when they were children.

Many cupcake critics say that the current cupcake craze is just a fad. But just ask anyone who has ever taken a big bite of one. Children and adults are crazy about cupcakes.

Answer the questions about the reading.

1. According to the reading, how does the *Oxford Companion to Food* define a cupcake?

_____

2. Place a check next to the two popular theories about the origin of the cupcake.

    a. _____ They were named after their inventor.

    b. _____ They were named after the way their ingredients were measured.

    c. _____ They were named after the pans they were baked in.

    d. _____ They were named after the small cakes people made for children.

3. The author chose interesting words when writing this story. One example is the alliteration in the phrase *current cupcake craze*. Make up another alliteration using the word *cupcake.*

_____

_____

4. The author also used similes, which are a way to compare two things using the words *like* or *as*. Write the sentence in the reading that includes a simile.

_____

5. Underline the differences between the way cupcakes were baked years ago and the way they are baked today.

    They look different today.

    They were once baked individually and now they can be baked in tins of twelve.

    They are made with different frostings now.

    They come in more varieties today.

6. What do many people say is the reason why they love cupcakes?

_____

7. Cupcakes are *intricately* decorated. That means they are _____.

    plain   very ornate   stale   very light

8. Do you like cupcakes? Why or why not?

_____

9. When Ann Warren says that she uses colors, shapes, and floral arrangements as inspiration, that means she uses those things to help her get ideas for her cupcakes. *True* or *false*?

_____

10. A critic is someone who judges something and may make a harsh comment. What do critics say about the current cupcake craze?_____

Food Critic for a Day

You are a food critic for your local newspaper. You and a friend went to The Greasy Spoon, a popular restaurant, to assess the food. After you ate, you returned to your computer and wrote your opinion of the meal.

For lunch, you had a small green salad with tomatoes and cucumbers. The salad dressing was creamy Italian. Then you ate a hamburger smothered in cheese, and a side order of sweet potato fries. You drank a chocolate milkshake with the meal. After you finished, you ordered a small slice of cheesecake.

Write your food review. Try to describe the aspects of the food you liked, as well as the parts you didn't like. Advise whether others should eat at The Greasy Spoon.

_____

_____

_____

_____

_____

_____

_____

_____

_____

_____

_____

_____

_____

I'd Like to Thank...

People are often given awards for doing things that help other people. They are also awarded for contributing to society. Scientists, writers, politicians, doctors, and teachers are often recognized for their work.

Write something you are talented at doing. _____

Now describe an appropriate award. _____

You are invited to receive your award at an extravagant ceremony in Los Angeles. The people who are giving you the honor would like for you to say a few words about yourself and the reason why you received the award. The speech should be short, but long enough to thank people who have inspired and helped you and to explain how you became so talented at what you do.

Write your speech here.

_____

_____

_____

_____

_____

_____

_____

_____

_____

_____

Practice your speech until you would be comfortable giving it to an audience. Pay attention to punctuation and use good expression. You don't want to put anyone to sleep!

Telescope in Space

For hundreds of years, astronomers have looked up at the sky and wondered. They have asked themselves questions like "How old is the universe?" and "How are planets formed?" Thanks to the scientists at the National Aeronautics and Space Administration, or NASA, these questions have been answered by one of the greatest advances in space exploration: the Hubble Space Telescope.

Launched into space in 1990, the space telescope orbits earth. In its voyage around our planet, it photographs pictures and sends detailed information and images back down to astronomers. The data and photos have helped scientists understand how galaxies form. They have even been able to narrow down the age of the universe to between 13 and 14 billion years old.

There are more than 6,000 published scientific articles about the Hubble telescope and the data and photographs it has sent back to Earth. For example, the Hubble has documented clumps of gas and dust surrounding young stars, which clue astronomers into how new planets are formed. It has also sent photos of gamma-ray bursts, or peculiar and powerful energy explosions in space that occur when giant stars crash into each other. But these are just two examples of the countless observations that the Hubble makes.

The Hubble telescope orbits the earth in 97 minutes, traveling at about five miles per second. If the telescope had wheels it could go from New York to California in about 10 minutes. That's normally about a two-day drive, without stopping! Using a group of mirrors, the telescope captures light and directs it to special instruments designed to collect information about the universe in different ways. Some instruments search for planets, and others collect temperature readings and motion. Cameras photograph what the telescope sees and sensors keep it moving in the right direction. The instruments aboard the Hubble are solar-powered. They convert sunlight into the electricity they need to function.

The telescope is controlled by the Flight Operations Team, a large staff of hundreds of engineers and scientists at the Goddard Space Flight Center in Greenbelt, Maryland. They give the Hubble directions and commands, receive the data sent to Earth, and archive, or collect and store, the information. According to HubbleSite, the Hubble Space Telescope's Internet site, the telescope sends enough information each week to fill about 18 DVDs.

Many scientists worldwide want to use the Hubble telescope for their research. They compete for timeslots by submitting proposals to a committee of experts who choose the ones they think will make the best use of the Hubble's time. Every year more than 1,000 proposals are sent in, but only 200 are selected.

Answer the questions about the reading.

1. The author's purpose for writing this passage is to _____.
   a. entertain   **b.** inform
   c. argue or persuade   **d.** teach someone how to do something

2. Who launched the Hubble Space Telescope?_____

3. Describe some of the things the telescope does.
_____
_____

4. It takes the Hubble telescope 10 minutes to orbit Earth. *True* or *false*? _____

5. How could you describe something that is solar-powered? _____
   a. It runs on gasoline.   **b.** It runs on batteries.
   c. It converts sunlight into electricity.   **d.** It uses its own power to create more energy.

6. Find a synonym in the reading for the word *information*. _____

7. Do you agree that the Hubble Space Telescope is one of the greatest advances in space exploration? Explain.
_____
_____

8. What does *archive* mean?
_____

9. If a typical DVD can hold up to 8 hours of video information, about how many hours of data does the Hubble collect in a week? _____

10. About how many scientists are able to use the Hubble for their research each year?
_____

What's New, Kitty-Cat?

Cats purr, meow, yowl, chatter, chirp, hiss, and growl. They use their tails, ears, whiskers, and eyes to communicate with their owners and show them how they feel. Sometimes they use both sounds and movements at the same time. One study conducted at Cornell University in Ithaca, New York, found that cats communicate in hundreds of ways. But what exactly do all of those noises and movements mean?

Cats don't meow at other cats. A meow is the way a cat talks to its owner and can mean anything from "Hi, I'm glad to see you," to "Hey, I'm hungry." When cats wait for someone to look in their direction and then mouth a silent meow, it means they are politely requesting a treat or a yummy snack. Just make sure to step back and leave the cat alone when he or she hisses or spits. That usually means "Leave me alone."

Cats also use their bodies to communicate. A cat who marches into a room with its tail flying high means "I'm really happy to see you." If that tail starts to wag or thrash back and forth, it means "back off." Unlike dogs, whose wagging tails mean they are excited and happy, a wagging cat tail is a sign of agitation. Tails that flick indicate that the cat is disappointed about something. Perhaps your cat was expecting someone else? Not to worry, cats are loyal to their owners. They show it by rubbing their bodies or heads against your legs and by something animal researchers call a "kitty kiss."

Just one way in which cats show affection, a cat gives a kitty kiss when he or she slowly blinks his or her eyes in your direction. That means you are the recipient of the cat's affection. It means "I love you so much." Cats also use their ears to show how much they like you. For example, ears that are facing forward and tilted back a little mean that the cat is feeling relaxed and friendly. Whiskers that are extended forward also mean that the cat is interested in you or what you might be doing. These are the times to talk to and play with your cat.

There are also a few things cats do to let you know they are not in the mood to play. For example, ears and whiskers that are back and lying flat mean that the cat is fearful and defensive, or ready to fight.

Cats communicate with people all the time. The next time a cat walks toward you with its tail in the air, smile and say hi back.

Answer the questions about the reading.

1. The main idea of this reading is that cats _____.

    a. like to be scratched and held   **b.** communicate in many different ways

    c. are independent   **d.** are entertaining pets to have around

2. Cats meow at other cats all the time. *True* or *false*? _____

3. Label what a cat is feeling when its tail looks like this.

3. _____

4. Label what a cat is feeling when its ears and whiskers are doing this.

4. _____

5. How do cats show their loyalty to their owners?

_____

Match each behavior to its meaning.

silent meowing	I love you.
hissing or spitting	I'm hungry.
tail thrashing back and forth	I'm fearful and defensive.
kitty kissing	Leave me alone.
ears and whiskers back and lying flat	Back off.

To Blog or Not to Blog

Should I blog or not? That is the question many young people are asking themselves. How can you blog safely, writing about your own life in a place where many people you don't know will read it?

Blogs are the fastest growing trend on the Internet. Blogs are personal diaries, or daily accounts of what is going on in someone's life. It can contain anything the blogger, or author, wants to include, such as pictures, recipes, news, poems, stories, and thoughts. Thousands of people of all ages blog each day.

Blog stands for "Web-log." A Web-log is a casual and personal Web site. The word itself is both a noun and a verb. For example, you can *blog*, which means "write." You can also write your thoughts in a blog.

Most often, a blog is a website with dated entries written by one person. Sometimes a blogger will include links to other people's blogs. Some of the earliest blogs were merely lists of cool information the author found and wanted to share with others. Soon these bloggers began adding commentary, or their opinions. Then they started posting their blogs every day. As more and more people read and left comments on a blogger's Web page, he or she would begin to read other people's blogs. Soon a community was formed.

At the end of 1999, special computer software was invented. This blogging software gave anyone the ability to post content, or place his or her blog on a website. Today, free blogging software is available to anyone who wants to download and use it. By posting information on the Internet, everyone gets a chance to say what they want to say.

Blogs are also a way to get valuable information quickly. Written in interesting ways, blogs could actually save you time. Because bloggers who write about the same subjects tend to read each other's work, the best advice tends to be repeated in numerous places. You could open a blog or two and find the same recommendation written in two different ways by two different people.

Another advantage of blogs is that they are very current with what is going on in the world. Many people check their favorite blogs before reading the news. That's because many bloggers write and comment about current and local events.

Blogs are here to stay. If you are interested in starting your own blog, remember that the Internet can also be a scary place. The important thing to remember is to leave out information that is too personal.

Answer the questions about the reading.

1. What is the word *blog* a shortened form of? _____

2. A blog is a(n) _____.
    a. Web site that sells comic books
    b. online diary where people share thoughts and opinions
    c. computer program that teaches people to type
    d. reference website to look up information

3. Circle all the words in the word bank that describe what people include in their blogs.

> poems   news   home address   thoughts   stories
> telephone number   photos   recipes   name of school

4. Why do you think people should never include in a blog their home address, telephone number, and name of the school they attend?

_____

5. Use the word *blog* as a noun in a sentence. _____

_____

6. Use the word *blog* as a verb in a sentence. _____

_____

7. If you were looking for information about a new restaurant and wanted someone's opinion, would you look on a blog? _____

8. If you wanted information for a report you have to write for school, would you look on a blog?

_____

9. Circle two advantages of blogs.
    They contain up-to-date information.
    They are boring to read.
    They are good places to buy used video games and books.
    They are good ways to get others' opinions.

10. If you were going to write a blog about yourself, what would you include?

_____

A Slice of History

It comes plain or with pepperoni, pineapple, or peppers. It can be round or square. It can be thin and crusty or thick and doughy. Whatever your preference, pizza is about as American as baseball and apple pie. Or is it? While millions of pizzas are consumed by Americans every day, the true origin of this delectable feast began in Italy.

In the late 1800s, an Italian baker in Naples, Italy, created a new recipe for a visiting king and queen. This baker, Raffaele Esposito, wanted to share his patriotism and impress the guests of his town. He did that by topping a flat round bread with foods whose colors represented the Italian flag. The ingredients he chose to use were red tomato, white mozzarella cheese, and green basil. After tasting Raffaele's creation, the king and queen were so impressed that word quickly spread throughout the village. Other bakers began copying the recipe and the rest is history.

Pizza traveled to America at the beginning of the 1900s. At that time, many of the people who immigrated to this country brought the culture and food of their homelands. Italian people brought their pizza recipe.

Because many Italian immigrants settled in New York City and Chicago, small cafes in both cities began serving Italian favorites. Pizza was one of them. During World War II in the 1940s, many American soldiers stationed on the Italian border were exposed to pizza. When they returned home, pizza was popular with them.

Pizza is a simple dish made of four basic ingredients. The crust is the base of the pizza. It is usually made from wheat flour, but it can also be made from whole wheat or bleached flour. On top is the sauce. Tomato based and sprinkled with spices, the sauce is spooned onto the crust and spread all over it. Cheese is probably one of the best parts of pizza. Grated mozzarella cheese has traditionally been the cheese used in pizza making, but other varieties of cheese work, too. The fourth ingredient on a pizza is the topping.

What people like on their pizzas ranges from pepperoni, sausage, and mushrooms to barbecue chicken, ham, and pineapple slices. Pizza is all about personal preference. Just like toppings, pizza style also varies. For example, a New York-style pizza has a thin crust which is made by tossing it in the air and whirling it around. Chicago-style pizza crust is much thicker.

Whether you like it thin or thick, covered with mushrooms or meatballs, pizza is currently one of the most popular food choices in America.

Answer the questions about the reading.

1. Why did Raffaele Esposito use red, white, and green foods on the first pizza?

_____

2. The word _immigrated_ in paragraph 3 means _____.
    a. learned to make pizza
    b. came to one country from another
    c. spread good news from town to town
    d. born in a country

3. A person born in one country who comes to another one to live is called an

_____.

4. What two cities were home to the first pizza parlors in America? _____

_____

5. The four main ingredients in pizza are _____.
    a. sauce, cheese, pepperoni, and parsley
    b. crust, cheese, broccoli, and mushrooms
    c. sauce, crust, sausages, and spices
    d. crust, sauce, cheese, and toppings

6. Number the pizza-making steps in the correct order.
    _____ Spread sauce over the crust.
    _____ Sprinkle grated mozzarella cheese over the sauce.
    _____ Flatten the crust into a round or square pan.
    _____ Add toppings.

7. Describe the difference between New York-and Chicago-style pizza.

_____

8. How did soldiers who returned to America after World War II know about pizza? _____
    a. They read about it in the newspaper.
    b. They tasted it while stationed on the Italian border.
    c. Their families told them about pizza.
    d. They didn't know about pizza until they got back home.

9. The effect is what happens and the cause explains why. Complete the Cause and Effect chart below.

Cause	Effect
Raffaele Esposito wanted to impress the king and queen.	
	Small cafes began selling Italian food.

Three Days of History

In July 1863, there was a battle in Pennsylvania where thousands of men fought and died for what they believed in. The land on which these men fought more than 145 years ago is regarded and respected by the two million people who visit the battle site each year.

The site of the Battle of Gettysburg, one of the most famed battles of the Civil War, has been preserved and is open to anyone who loves history. The national park covers 5,989 acres and has more than 40 miles of scenic paths that twist and wind past open fields and engraved markers. Visitors to the site are awed by the enormity of the bravery displayed there, including more than 1,000 monuments and cannons.

Gettysburg is America's largest battlefield shrine. It places visitors right where men fought. It points out the exact spots where smaller battles were won. It highlights the place where President Abraham Lincoln spoke. People go there to learn, to remember, and to honor the heroism and valor of the soldiers who protected what they believed in: freedom.

Visitors to Gettysburg can witness living history. That means they can visit an encampment to talk to and see how a Civil War soldier is dressed, inspect where he sleeps, and smell what he eats while it cooks. Tourists can watch a re-enactment of an actual battle. They see flags waving and hear horses thundering through the fields, cannons bursting, and rifles cracking. They are able to witness battle scenarios that bring to life the actual battles that took place there on July 1, 2, and 3, 1863.

Thousands of re-enactors, or men and women who recreate characters from historic events, play the roles of both Union and Confederate soldiers. Authenticity is very important to re-enactors. They dedicate themselves to dressing in period clothing, carrying authentic-looking weaponry, and living as closely as possible to the way people during 1863 would have lived. Many re-enactors spend hundreds of hours training and learning about history. They spend thousands of dollars on clothes and other items to help them look and act genuine.

The site houses ten Civil War–related museums that are filled with artifacts and information about the battles. There are tours of an authentic Civil War house, as well as a live theater that hosts a "President Lincoln" and a group that performs plays. In real life, President Lincoln visited Gettysburg just four months after the battles and he dedicated the battlefield as a National Cemetery. It was there he spoke for two minutes, delivering his famous Gettysburg Address.

Answer the questions about the reading.

1. The Battle of Gettysburg took place on _____ and was the most famed battle of the _____ War.

2. The Gettysburg National Park is America's largest battlefield *shrine*. Another word for *shrine* is

_____.

memorial   park   re-enactment   school

3. Why do people visit places like Gettysburg today?

_____

4. Underline the sentence in the reading that defines what a re-enactor is.

5. Please check next to all the things that Civil War re-enactors do to look and act authentic.
   a. ____ train and learn about history
   b. ____ dress in costume but prefer not to act appropriately
   c. ____ dress in period clothing
   d. ____ live as closely as they can to the way people did in 1863

6. Write a sentence describing *living history*.

_____

_____

7. Find the word *encampment* in the reading. What is the root word? _____
What do you think *encampment* means? _____

_____

8. List two things that visitors to Gettysburg can do.

_____ and _____

9. Does it seem like the author ever visited Gettysburg? Why or why not?

_____

10. After reading this, do you think you would like to go to the Gettysburg National Park? Explain what makes you feel that way.

_____

_____

Fact or Opinion?

A fact is something that is true. It is known to have occurred, to exist, or to be actual. An example of a fact is:

> The Declaration of Independence was signed in 1776.

An opinion is a person's view about a particular issue. It is what the person believes or thinks. It is not necessarily the truth. Here's an example of an opinion:

> My neighbor is the best neighbor in the world.

Write *F* or *O* next to each sentence to tell whether it is fact or opinion.

1. _____ Boston is in Massachusetts.

2. _____ The Giants are the best football team in the world.

3. _____ Every time Michael washes his car, it ends up raining.

4. _____ Whales are mammals.

5. _____ John F. Kennedy was elected President of the United States in 1961.

6. _____ The Harry Potter books are better than the movies.

7. _____ Dogs are more lovable than cats.

8. _____ My father bought his car in 2006.

9. _____ Lance Armstrong won seven Tour de France races.

10. _____ Hot dogs taste better at a baseball game than hamburgers do.

Idioms: Strange Sayings

An idiom is an expression whose meaning is difficult to figure out from the meanings of the separate words that make up the phrase. To find out what an idiom means, it is important to use context clues, or the words that surround it. The following paragraph contains an idiom:

Jan's teacher explained the math assignment one more time. Jan still didn't understand. To her, the directions were as **clear as mud**.

In that final sentence, *clear as mud* is an idiom. In reading it, we see that Jan doesn't understand her teacher's directions. To Jan, the directions are confusing and unclear. The idiom *clear as mud* must mean "confusing and unclear."

Use context clues to figure out the boldfaced idioms used below. Write the meaning.

1. Thomas and Matt were on their way to the soccer game. Thomas was being very quiet and seemed like he was lost in thought. "Hey, **a penny for your thoughts**," said Matt.

   _____

2. Emily felt cranky at school. Everything anyone said to her seemed all wrong. I must have **gotten up on the wrong side of bed this morning,** she thought. _____

   _____

3. The score was tied in the baseball game and Joe decided to **pull out all the stops**. He stepped up to the plate, determined to hit a home run. _____

   _____

4. Despite Nicole's hard work, she still didn't win the contest. Her mom knew how disappointed she was feeling. **"That's the way the cookie crumbles,"** said Mom. _____

   _____

5. Everything is more fun when Uncle Jimmy comes to visit our house. He laughs and jokes all the time. My father says he's **a barrel of laughs**. _____

   _____

How Old Is That Rock?

When you think about rocks, you probably do not think about when those rocks celebrate their birthdays. But some scientists who study rocks spend a lot of their time trying to find out when rocks were born, or first formed.

Rocks and What They Tell Us

Rocks are solid, natural aggregates, which are mixtures of minerals. Scientists study rocks to uncover what they are made of. A rock's composition is important in determining the age of the rock. When scientists know how old a rock is, then they learn more about what earth was like that many years ago.

Every single rock contains a clue about earth's history. Rocks carry with them the evidence of the events that formed them. When scientists examine rocks, they use those clues to learn more about how our planet was formed. Each type of scientist uses a different method to determine a rock's age. Geologists study the history, origin, and structure of the earth. They use a method called relative time. Paleontologists use fossils to get information. Geochemists, scientists who study the chemical changes in the earth's crust, examine radioactive decay to determine the age of a rock.

Relative Time

In 1815, an engineer named William Smith collected rocks and discovered that certain layers of earth contain specific types of rocks and fossils. He used this discovery to create diagrams that show layers of rock. Following the assumption that older rocks are found underneath younger ones, he was able to determine the age of a rock type, relative to others above or below it.

Fossils

Paleontologists use a time scale developed by early scientists that show which animals and plants lived during certain prehistoric periods. By examining a fossil and then determining the animal or plant that left such an imprint, a paleontologist can pinpoint the general age of the rock.

Atomic Clocks

Using radioactive elements in rocks, called atomic clocks, geochemists are able to calculate when they were formed. These scientists use a special instrument called a Geiger counter to find out how much radioactive material is in a rock. By comparing this information with time scales, they can figure out exactly when the rock was born. By this method they also learn when that part of earth's surface was created.

Answer the questions about the reading.

1. Some nonficition readings use headings to help organize the material and make it easier to read and understand. Which of the following is **not** a heading in this reading? _____

  a. Fossils   **b.** Atomic Clocks

  c. Rocks Are Heavy   **d.** Rocks and What They Tell Us

2. Circle the reasons why scientists study rocks.

      to find out what they are composed of

      to see how far they can be thrown

      to see how old they are

      to learn more about Earth

3. Another word for *clue* in paragraph 3 is _____.

4. Paleontologists study _____ to determine the age of rocks.

5. The instrument that geochemists use to measure the amount of radioactive material in a rock is called a _____.

6. Read the following paragraph. Circle the sentence that is an opinion.

> Scientists use rocks to help learn more about the earth. Paleontologists use fossils to find out the age of the rocks they are in. Rocks are much more interesting than fossils.

7. William Smith studied the earth's layers. *True* or *false*? _____

8. Under which heading would you look to find information about what we can learn from rocks?

_____

9. Read this generalization: All rocks help us learn about the earth's history. After reading the passage, do you agree? _____

10. Circle the sentence in the reading that supports the generalization above.

The Birthday Cake

Everything was perfect. The decorations were up. The cake was in the oven. The guests were expected to arrive in one hour. Lisa looked around and smiled. She had been planning her birthday party for more than two months and it was finally here.

The theme of Lisa's party was Rock Star. All of her friends watched the popular television show on which regular people performed and were assessed by a panel of judges. The karaoke machine was set up, and when everyone got there, Lisa's mother started the fun. "Who's our first contestant?"

Kristina jumped up and down. She loved to sing and dance and knew exactly what song she was going to sing. After each girl took her turn to perform, Lisa's mother set the table for cake and ice cream. Lisa thought that the cake looked absolutely perfect. She was so pleased that she had made it herself. She watched as her friends sampled it.

"Um, hmmm," smiled Stephanie, awkwardly. "This is interesting."

Jessica looked at Lisa and tried to hide the fact that there was something wrong. "Mmmm, delicious," she choked out.

Lisa was surprised that her friends didn't seem to like the cake she made. She took a big forkful and put it into her mouth. It tasted salty and bitter. She looked up at her guests and everyone had the same expression on their faces. They all looked at Lisa to see what she would do. At that moment, Lisa's mother came into the dining room to see how the party was going. She took one look around and knew something was not right.

"Taste the cake, Mom," said Lisa quietly. Lisa's mom took a piece. She knew exactly what was wrong the second she tasted it. She walked into the kitchen and brought out two similar canisters in different sizes.

"Which one of these containers did you take the sugar out of?" she asked Lisa.

Lisa pointed to the smaller one. Her mother opened it and walked over to her. Lisa dipped her finger into the tin and tasted. It was salt. "Oh, no," said Lisa, laughing. "I put salt in the cake instead of sugar!"

Lisa looked at her friends. They were smiling. At first she thought they were going to make fun of her, but then Jessica looked at her and said, "Do we have to finish our cake?"

Lisa and the girls burst out laughing. Her mother collected the plates and brought out ice cream sundaes. As she sat and watched her friends having a good time, Lisa realized that this is what real friends do. *They still like me even though I made a mistake*, she thought. Lisa smiled. That discovery was perhaps her best birthday gift that year.

Answer the questions about the story.

1. Why do you think the author wrote this story?

_____

2. A synonym for the word *canister* is _____.
  a. cake plate   **b.** container   **c.** tablecloth   **d.** karaoke machine

3. Number the events of the story in the correct order.
  _____ Lisa realized how wonderful her friends are.
  _____ Everyone got a chance to perform.
  _____ Lisa's mother brought out the canisters.
  _____ After tasting the cake, Lisa knew something was wrong.

4. What is a *contestant*?

_____

5. How do you explain why Lisa mistook the salt for sugar?

_____

_____

6. How do you think Lisa felt right after she discovered her mistake?

_____

7. What lesson is the story trying to teach? _____
  a. Making mistakes is a terrible thing.
  b. Birthdays should be perfect.
  c. Good friends overlook mistakes and like us for who we are.
  d. Baking is a difficult thing to do and should never be done without an adult.

8. The effect is what happens and the cause explains why. Complete the Cause and Effect chart below.

Cause	Effect
Lisa's mother asked, "Who's our first contestant?"	
	The cake tasted salty and bitter.

No More Tears

The average American eats about 20 pounds of onions every year. They come in three varieties: yellow, red, and white. Onions are a good source of vitamin C, potassium, fiber, and folic acid. They also contain calcium, iron, and antioxidants that are good for the heart. But peeling onions has always made people cry. Thanks to a combination of biology and technology, however, that doesn't have to happen anymore.

Scientists in New Zealand and Japan worked together to create an onion that won't make people cry when they cut it. Using biotechnology, these scientists found the gene that was responsible for all the tears and they silenced it.

In the human body, genes are parts of DNA that contain instructions for cells making proteins. Genes live in chromosomes. Every cell has chromosomes, and therefore every cell has DNA and genes. The cells make proteins that are copied and sent to do their jobs, which include keeping our bodies running well. A damaged gene gets the instructions wrong. Scientists in Australia discovered that a gene can even be "silenced" not to do its job at all.

Here is how the concept can work in a onion. Cutting into an onion releases onion oil. This oil contains an acid that makes eyes water. People aren't actually crying when they peel onions; their eyes are merely watering. The scientists used gene-silencing to switch off the genes in the onion that produce the acidic chemical in the oil. They blocked those particular genes so that the tears will stop.

The scientists who located and silenced that gene in onions believe that they are making life better for people who love the vegetable. One researcher from New Zealand said that the scientists are hoping the process will also improve the taste of the onion. Without the bitter and strong sensation caused when someone peels an onion, scientists believe that the onion's natural sweet aromas will be the only scent that reaches the nose.

The project is in its beginning stages, but it is an exciting one. The idea has caused a lot of enthusiasm throughout the world. The researchers are working to make sure that the tearless onions can be grown efficiently. Currently they are developing some model onion plants but don't expect to be able to place a "no tears" onion on every dinner table for another 10 to 15 years.

Answer the questions about the reading.

1. This informational reading is composed mostly of facts. Find the author's opinion and circle that sentence.

2. When people cut into onions, they are not really crying. *True* or *false*? _____

3. According to the reading, *genes* are ____.
   a. not responsible for causing people to cry when peeling onions
   b. parts of DNA that contain instructions
   c. a source of vitamin C and fiber
   d. silent

4. Gene-silencing was first discovered by scientists in _____.

5. Why do you think scientists want to create a "no tears" onion?
_____

_____

6. How many years will pass before tearless onions will be available in stores? ____
   a. 5 to 10   **b.** 20   **c.** 10 to 15   **d.** 2 to 3

7. Number the events in the correct order.
   ____ Your eyes begin to water.
   ____ You cut into an onion.
   ____ The onion produces an oil.
   ____ An acid in the oil irritates your eyes.

8. Think about a fruit or vegetable that you would like to see changed in some way. For example, maybe you think that broccoli should taste better. Write your idea below and explain why you think the fruit or vegetable you chose should be improved.

_____

_____

_____

_____

All Eyes on Phil

Punxsutawney, Pennsylvania, is a quiet little town. The people who live there work, go to school, and shop just like anyone else who lives in a small town in America. But when February approaches, this tiny village is transformed into a bustling, or busy, <u>metropolis</u> complete with crowds and traffic. The busy streets and packed sidewalks are all thanks to Punxsutawney Phil.

Punxsutawney Phil is the most famous groundhog in the United States. Early in the morning of February 2 each year, all eyes are on Phil. That's because he has been coaxed out of his warm hole and into the chill. Phil's job is to let the country know just how much more winter is to come that year.

If Phil sees his shadow, then winter will be sticking around for six more weeks. But if he doesn't see his shadow, spring is supposedly just around the corner. While not many people can remember how this tradition got started, most everyone who travels to Gobbler's Knob in Punxsutawney is visiting to see what Phil has to say. But how many people know that Punxsutawney Phil is not the only weather-predicting groundhog in this country?

Buckeye Chuck lives in Marion, Ohio. Since the 1970s, he has been predicting the arrival of spring every year. Like Phil, he hibernates from late September to early April. But on February 2, Chuck is pulled from his burrow to check out his shadow. Or not.

People in Alabama look to Smith Lake Jake, a groundhog that lives at the Birmingham Zoo in Birmingham, for their answers. He, too, makes an appearance on Groundhog Day. The only difference between Jake and some of his peers is that southern groundhogs like to sleep in. Jake does his annual job at around 10 AM.

At the Staten Island Zoo in New York City, Staten Island Chuck not only ventures out and predicts the weather on Groundhog Day, but this perky mammal makes guest appearances throughout the day at the zoo. He even attends a breakfast and a blood drive.

The legend of Groundhog Day dates back to an old Scottish poem that goes like this: "If Candlemas Day is bright and clear, there'll be two winters in that year." Candlemas Day came before Groundhog Day. It was celebrated in the 1700s when German settlers arrived in Pennsylvania. The holiday fell between winter and spring. German tradition states that if the weather was nice on Candlemas Day, then the second half of winter would be cold and stormy. In other words, if the sun came out on February 2—allowing a groundhog to see its shadow—there would be six more weeks of winter.

Answer the questions about the reading.

1. Circle the synonyms for *metropolis* in the word bank.

> city   hamlet   village   hub   small town   capital

2. Find a word in the reading that means *busy*. _____

3. Explain why Punxsutawney Phil is the most famous groundhog in the United States.

_____

_____

4. Circle the idiom* in this sentence from the passage: *But if he doesn't see his shadow, spring is supposedly just around the corner.*

5. Explain what the idiom above means.

_____

_____

6. Punxsutawney Phil is the only weather-predicting groundhog in America.
True or *false*? _____

7. What is so special about Staten Island Chuck? _____
   a. He sleeps late.
   b. He makes guest appearances at the zoo on Groundhog Day.
   c. He hibernates all winter and wakes up in the spring every year.
   d. He sometimes refuses to come out of his burrow.

8. One thing all weather-predicting groundhogs have in common is that they _____

_____.

9. If six more weeks of winter is the effect, what is the cause? _____
   a. Phil sees his shadow on February 2.
   b. Phil doesn't see his shadow on February 2.
   c. Phil sleeps in and doesn't come out of his burrow.
   d. Phil comes out and sleeps outside his burrow.

10. Do you think that using a groundhog to predict the weather is reliable? Why or why not?

_____

_____

* An idiom is an expression that has figurative meaning.

Make Boring Better

Boring sentences make reading, well, boring. Many authors find ways to spice up their stories by choosing interesting words and varying the length of the sentences they write. Sometimes writers add adjectives and adverbs. Sometimes they add more details.

Read this sentence: *The cat fell asleep.* It's boring, right? How can you improve it? Without changing the meaning of the sentence, you can add words that transform that boring sentence into an interesting one: *The tired cat drifted quickly off to sleep.*

Rewrite the following sentences so that they are more interesting for readers.

1. Stan jumped into the pool.

_____

2. The bird fell out of its nest in the tree.

_____

3. My best friend is a nice person.

_____

4. The dog wagged his tail.

_____

5. My sister likes cake.

_____

Smile, It's a Simile

A simile compares two things by using the words *like* or *as*. For example, *as strong as an ox* is a simile. Read each numbered sentence. Circle the simile in each sentence. Then circle the sentence below it that best describes what the simile means. By the way, this exercise may seem as hard as nails, but it's really as easy as pie.

1. My grandmother's hair is like white snow.
   a. Her hair is cold like snow.
   b. Her hair is the same color as snow.
   c. Her hair is not white.

2. Under the warm blankets, the baby was as snug as a bug in a rug.
   a. There were bugs in the bed.
   b. The baby was cozy under the blankets.
   c. The bed was uncomfortable and cold.

3. After scrubbing the kitchen floor, it was as clean as a whistle.
   a. The floor was still wet.
   b. The floor was covered with whistles.
   c. The floor was very clean.

4. The old pillow on the chair is like a flat pancake.
   a. The pillow is very flat.
   b. The pillow is fluffy and soft.
   c. The pillow is covering the chair.

5. The house my grandfather built in the 1940s is as solid as a rock.
   a. The house is falling apart.
   b. The house is sturdy and strong.
   c. The house is heavy and big.

What Does NASA Do?

Throughout the 1960s and 1970s, America's space program played a large role in what families watched together on television. Whole families would gather around the one television set they owned and watch breathlessly as the rocket launched from its pad, tore off its base, and blasted into outer space. Every minute was played out and Americans were there to see it. But times have changed and so has the space program. However, one thing has remained the same throughout the years: NASA's mission.

The National Aeronautics and Space Administration, or NASA, has been working for about 50 years to learn more about what is out in space. Its mission is to lead the way in scientific discovery and aeronautics research. Its main goal is to explore space.

Established in 1958 by U.S. President Dwight D. Eisenhower, NASA quickly became more and more popular. President John F. Kennedy spent a lot of time talking about and promoting space exploration. His focus was to send astronauts to the moon by the end of the 1960s. The Mercury and Gemini projects gave NASA the confidence to do just that. On July 20, 1969, NASA sent Apollo 11 to the moon. On that mission, astronauts Neil Armstrong and Buzz Aldrin were the first of 12 men to walk on the moon.

In addition, NASA scientists developed the first weather and communications satellites. Then in 1981, the Space Shuttle was launched for the first time. A reusable ship that gave NASA astronauts regular access to space, the shuttle has completed more than 120 successful flights since then. The International Space Station was built and brought together the work of 16 nations, including the United States. It has given us a permanent human presence in space since 2000.

The accomplishments of NASA scientists have often resulted in improvements to life here on earth. Some of the biggest innovations in America have come out of the space program. Just a few examples are cell phones, intensive care and heart monitoring equipment, and an international search and rescue system which helps emergency workers locate ships, planes, or people in trouble. Equipment to diagnose cancer and manage wildfires are also direct results of NASA research. Even Lifeshears, a handheld rescue tool that can cut through cars to free people who may be  trapped inside a car after an accident, was developed by NASA, which used a similar tool to separate rocket boosters from space shuttles. NASA plans to continue moving forward. Some of its plans include robotic missions to the moon and developing a way for regular people to go out into space like astronauts do.

Answer the questions about the reading.

1. NASA has been working for about _____ years to explore space.

2. NASA's mission is to _____.
    a. build a city on the moon
    b. lead the way in scientific discovery and space research
    c. keep track of how many falling stars are in the sky
    d. never go up into space

3. A timeline shows the events in a reading in a way that is easy to understand. Complete the following timeline.

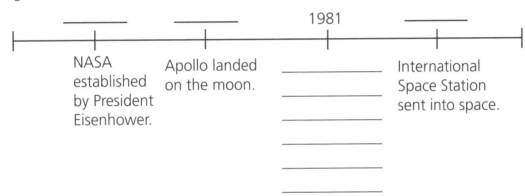

                                       1981

NASA established by President Eisenhower.   Apollo landed on the moon.   _____ _____ _____ _____ _____   International Space Station sent into space.

4. Another word for *innovation* in the last paragraph is _____ _____.
   invention   spaceship   gadget   satellite

5. Three innovations that came out of the space program are cell phones, heart monitoring equipment, and Lifeshears. *True* or *false*? _____

6. Which two space programs came before the Apollo program? Circle them both.

        Gemini   Comet   Space Shuttle program   Mercury

I Want Chocolate!

Did you know that chocolate is America's favorite flavor? According to a recent poll, 52 percent of adults in the United States claim to like chocolate more than any other flavor. Whether you prefer chocolate bars, candies, or drinks, chocolate has been in many people's lives for many years.

The first recorded history of chocolate dates back 2,000 years to Central America. There the Maya created a beverage out of crushed cacao beans and drew pictures of cocoa pods on the walls of their stone temples. Back then, cacao was held in high regard and enjoyed only by royalty at their sacred ceremonies.

Like the Maya, the Aztecs revered the cacao bean. They named their cocoa beverage *chocolatl*, which means "warm liquid." Historians believe that Aztec monarch Montezuma II filled huge storehouses with cacao beans and drank more than 50 goblets of chocolatl every day. Back then, cacao beans were also used as a form of currency. For example, an Aztec man could buy a rabbit for four cacao beans.

In 1502, Christopher Columbus brought a handful of almond-shaped beans from the Caribbean islands to Spain. He gave the dark beans to the King and Queen of Spain, who weren't very impressed. However, almost 20 years later the cacao bean made its comeback.

Hernando Cortes, a Spanish explorer, traveled to Mexico and discovered just how wonderful chocolate was. He experimented with the Aztec's chocolatl by adding sugar to make it sweeter. He also planted more cacao trees in the Caribbean. Back in Spain, spices like cinnamon and vanilla were added to the hot beverage. This was the birth of hot chocolate as we know it today.

Meanwhile, in America the first chocolate factory was built in 1765. The first box of chocolate was sold in 1854 and the first Tootsie Roll hit the candy store shelves in 1896. Hershey, Pennsylvania, was the birthplace of the first chocolate bar in 1900, and their famous chocolate Kisses wrapped in foil began selling in 1907.

The chocolate craze continued. Even the United States government believed strongly in the nutritional value of chocolate and ensured that its World War II troops had plenty of it. The chocolate bars gave the soldiers energy until they could get more food. Even in today's army meals, chocolate bars and chocolate candies are included. Chocolate has even been taken into space by astronauts. From bars to bunnies, chocolate seems to keep getting better and better. It's no wonder more than half of all Americans love it.

Answer the questions about the reading.

1. More than half of all Americans like chocolate better than any other flavor.
True or *false*? _____

2. Chocolate was first enjoyed as a _____ more than 2,000 years ago.
bar   candy Kiss   beverage   candy

3. The Aztecs named their chocolate beverage _____.

4. What does the word *currency* mean in paragraph 3? ____
   a. cacao beans   **b.** candy   **c.** money   **d.** meals

5. Number the following items in the correct order by the year they began being sold.
   ____ chocolate bars
   ____ Tootsie Rolls
   ____ chocolate Kisses
   ____ first box of chocolates

6. List ten things you know that are made of chocolate.
   _____
   _____

7. Circle the sentences in the reading that are the author's opinion.

8. Why do you think Hernando Cortes changed the way chocolatl tasted?
   _____
   _____

9. How do you think cacao beans taste? ____ Circle the sentence that is a clue.
   a. sweet   **b.** bitter   **c.** salty   **d.** spicy

10. What is your favorite flavor? Why?
   _____
   _____

The Flying Fish and the Dolphins

The Flying Fish, an unmanned aerial vehicle, or UAV, was developed by researchers in the aerospace engineering department at the University of Michigan. Powered by electricity, the seaplane took off, flew, and landed 22 times while being tested off the coast of Monterey, California. The two-day trial gave researchers a chance to see the plane in action.

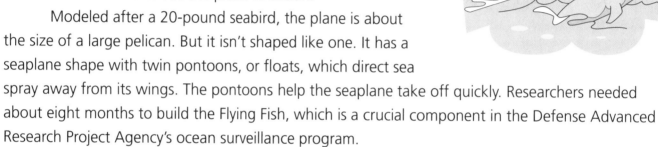

Modeled after a 20-pound seabird, the plane is about the size of a large pelican. But it isn't shaped like one. It has a seaplane shape with twin pontoons, or floats, which direct sea spray away from its wings. The pontoons help the seaplane take off quickly. Researchers needed about eight months to build the Flying Fish, which is a crucial component in the Defense Advanced Research Project Agency's ocean surveillance program.

One challenge that faced researchers was enabling the small plane to take off from the ocean. The vertical motion of waves poses a big dilemma for seaplanes. In this project, researers simply allowed the Flying Fish to crash through them during take-off.

Another challenge was ensuring that the seaplane could stay in its "watch circle," the defined space it is responsible for monitoring. During the trials, the Flying Fish needed to demonstrate that it could fly autonomously, or on its own, across its watch circle. It also had to prove that it could gather data while taking off, climbing to a designated altitude, cruising at that height, and then landing. Special onboard sensors measured the plane's speed. Researchers agreed that the tests were a success.

One surprising result of the seaplane's trial mission was the reaction of the dolphins living in the test area. Scientists saw dolphins swim over to the Flying Fish when it landed in the sea. The scientists aboard the mission's research ship said that the dolphins appeared to believe that the plane was a pelican diving for fish. When the dolphins discovered that the seaplane wasn't a pelican, they began playing with it! They swam in formation with the Flying Fish. They dove underneath it and swam from one side to the other.

The seaplane will be used to monitor animals and waves in the oceans. Apparently, it will also entertain some of the sea creatures who happen to live in its watch circle!

Answer the questions about the reading.

1. You know that the prefix *un-* means "not." You can figure out that the word *unmanned* means that ____.
   a. there was a pilot in the plane
   b. there was no pilot or crew in the plane
   c. the crew was untrained for the flight
   d. the plane flew across land, not water

2. The Flying Fish was modeled after a _____
   and is about the size of a large _____.

3. The Flying Fish looked exactly like a pelican. *True* or *false*? _____

4. Place a check next to the challenges researchers had to overcome.
   a. ____ taking off and landing in waves
   b. ____ making sure the plane stayed in its "watch circle"
   c. ____ rain and poor weather
   d. ____ seabirds

5. It was important that the Flying Fish could fly *autonomously*. What does that mean?
   _____

6. The seaplane's "watch circle" is the ____.
   a. circle near its wings that people like to watch
   b. area between the waves and the plane's wings
   c. place where the dolphins waited for the plane
   d. defined space that the plane is responsible for monitoring

7. The seaplane had special sensors onboard that measured how fast it was going.
   True or *false*? _____

8. How did the dolphins interact with the Flying Fish?
   _____

   _____

9. The seaplane is being tested so that it will be able to ____.
   a. play with dolphins
   b. monitor animals and waves in the ocean
   c. entertain children at science fairs
   d. capture fish and lobsters

10. Why do you think the dolphins were attracted to the seaplane?
    _____

Is It a Gross?
Or Is It Just Gross?

There are many words in the English language that mean more than one thing. One example is the word *gross*. Something that is repulsive is gross, such as in the sentence *That stinky cheese is gross.* But *gross* can also mean 144 of something, as in *The man bought a gross of limes.*

Use context clues to determine what the multiple-meaning words in bold mean. Then underline the correct definition.

1. The baseball **field** was covered with dandelions.
   a. to answer with skill
   b. to retrieve
   c. grassy area where sports are played

2. The shortstop ran toward second base to **field** the ball.
   a. to answer with skill
   b. to retrieve
   c. grassy area where sports are played

3. My teacher asked me to write a **report** about bees.
   a. a statement of a student's grades
   b. to communicate information
   c. a written document that describes something in detail

4. The journalist will **report** on the fire later.
   a. a statement of a student's grades
   b. to communicate information
   c. a written document that describes something in detail

5. I found a **quarter** on the ground and will use it to buy some gum.
   a. a coin that is worth one-fourth of a dollar
   b. one of four equal parts of anything
   c. to divide into four equal parts

6. My mother said she would **quarter** the apple.
   a. a coin that is worth one-fourth of a dollar
   b. one of four equal parts of anything
   c. to divide into four equal parts

The Write Way, Right?

Homophones are words that look different and have different meanings but are pronounced the same way. See how *write* and *right* are homonyms:

I love to *write* stories about my family.

I throw a baseball with my *right* hand.

Circle the homophones in each pairs of sentences below. Then answer the questions.

> She introduces her new beau to her parents.
> I put a bright red bow on top of the present.

1. Which homophone means "a male admirer"? _____

2. Which homophone means "a decorative knot"? _____

> The town's council met about the flooding on Main Street.
> The psychologist will counsel the family about their problem.

3. Which homophone means "to give advice" or "advise"? _____

4. Which homophone means "a group of people who meet for a purpose"? _____

> The miner worked to collect rocks and slate underground.
> The girl had a minor case of sunburn after being outside all day.

5. Which homophone means "less" or "smaller"? _____

6. Which homophone means "someone who works in a mine"? _____

> The queue became impatient while waiting for the store to open.
> If I don't know what a word means, I can look for a cue on the page.

7. Which homophone means "a hint that gives information about what to do next"?

_____

8. Which homophone means "a group of people waiting in a line"? _____

> In social studies class, we talk about current events.
> My grandmother likes to put a currant in her oatmeal in the morning.

9. Which homophone means something "that is happening now"? _____

10. Which homophone means "a small, dried, seedless fruit"? _____

A Real Jurassic Park?

How many times have you seen the movie *Jurassic Park* and wondered if scientists really could bring back dinosaurs? What would the world be like? Well, you don't have to worry or wonder any longer, and here is why.

Beth Shapiro is a scientist who studies and works with ancient DNA. She says that the concept behind *Jurassic Park* will always stay just a movie, because there is no way to bring back the dinosaurs. Based on the biochemistry of DNA, fragments that a dead animal leaves behind can survive for only about 100,000 years.

DNA is what makes you who you are. Everyone, including dinosaurs, has their own set of DNA. It contains all of the instructions to make your whole body. The DNA in your body, which is inside all of the genes in all of your cells, keeps your body working the way it should. DNA did the same thing for the dinosaurs.

In order to recreate the dinosaur-themed park that the movie takes place in, Shapiro says that DNA strands must be extraordinarily well preserved. The best environment for preserving DNA is very cold, very dry, and salty. For even a fragment of the DNA to be useable, conditions must be just right. In her search for the perfect DNA sample, Shapiro's research has led her team of scientists to frigid places like Siberia, Alaska, and the Yukon.

In those cold places, Shapiro has found bones from animals such as mammoths, steppe bison, and North American lions that lived during the last Ice Age. She tries to extract, or draw out, DNA sequences from the bones or the surrounding soil. She and the other scientists then examine the DNA to learn about what the animal's environment was like when it was alive.

After an animal dies, its DNA begins to break down immediately, and so the samples Shapiro acquires are usually not in good shape. The strands are damaged or broken and in such poor condition that she is unable to continue working with them. Furthermore, in order to recreate, for example, a mammoth, there must be adequate available quantities of a special type of DNA called mitochondrial DNA. This differs from regular DNA because mitochondrial DNA is what makes animals different from other animals. It is what sets each animal apart.

In human beings, the total amount of genetic information in their genes and DNA sequences is more than 300 billion parts. Most of the information that Shapiro extracts from the bones she finds add up to only about 100 to 200 parts. That's not enough genetic information to recreate an ancient animal. More DNA would have to be extracted somehow.

Shapiro doesn't envision that happening anytime soon. While scientists have indeed found insects and plants preserved in amber, just like the small insects in *Jurassic Park*, the movie will remain a movie.

Answer the questions about the reading.

1. The word *extracted* in paragraph 7 means ____.

    a. put back in   **b.** drawn out   **c.** ignored   **d.** cleaned out

2. What is Beth Shapiro's occupation? ____

    a. She is a doctor.   **b.** She is an engineer.

    c. She is a biologist.   **d.** She is a scientist.

3. DNA contains all the instructions to make your entire body. *True* or *false*? _____

4. Shapiro and her team have found bones from animals that lived during the last

    _____.

5. Number the events in the correct order.

    ____ The dinosaur's DNA begins to break down immediately.

    ____ Only a small amount of DNA is useable and Shapiro cannot make a dinosaur.

    ____ A dinosaur dies.

    ____ Shapiro and her team extract DNA from bones and surrounding soil.

6. Underline Shapiro's opinion about recreating the dinosaur-themed park in *Jurassic Park*.

    She thinks it is possible.

    She thinks it is a good idea and is studying how to do it.

    She doesn't think it is possible to make dinosaurs from DNA.

    She thinks *Jurassic Park* can be a reality.

7. DNA is best preserved in a hot and damp climate. *True* or *false*? _____

8. *Jurassic Park* was a great movie. *Fact* or *opinion*? _____

9. DNA helps keep our bodies working properly. *Fact* or *opinion*? _____

10. Shapiro studies ancient DNA. Another way to express *ancient* is ____.

    a. very old   **b.** tired   **c.** new   **d.** messy

Cruising Along

Many people love to go on cruises. There seems to be something special about standing on the deck of a huge ship in the middle of the ocean with the smell of salt water in your nose and the wind on your face. Cruise ships today boast jogging tracks, swimming pools, restaurants, and ballrooms. But cruise ships have not always been that luxurious.

The first transatlantic voyage took place in the 1400s. The ship, which crossed the Atlantic Ocean, was not nearly as majestic as cruise ships are today. Accommodations for passengers were far less stately, or grand. Then, in 1818, a New York shipping company called Black Ball Line began offering passenger service across the seas. The first ship built primarily for the purpose of cruising was the *Princess Victoria Luise*.

The *Victoria Luise* looked more like a private yacht than today's enormous cruise ships. She held 120 cabins, a library, gym, and a darkroom where photographers could develop their photographs. The 4,409-ton passenger ship was launched on January 10, 1900, and carried passengers until December 1906. That's when it was accidentally grounded, or driven onto the shore, off the coast of Jamaica.

As cruising became more popular, companies began competing for customers. Ships became bigger and better. They added more luxuries to attract vacationing travelers. One of the earliest and most famous ocean liners built and launched during the early 1900s was the *Titanic*.

The *Titanic* set out on its maiden, or first, voyage in spring of 1912. The passenger ship could hold more than 2,200 passengers. It weighed 46,328 tons and offered an onboard swimming pool, libraries, a gym, and elaborately decorated restaurants. But as it was crossing the Atlantic Ocean, the *Titanic* struck an iceberg on April 14. The ship sank the next day.

The cruise ship industry became less popular during the 1960s, when large passenger jets made air travel more convenient. But cruise ships are still enticing. Much like floating hotels, today's ocean liners offer water parks, coffee shops, rock-climbing walls, basketball courts, ice-skating rinks, and miniature golf courses. Passengers can play, shop, eat, and be entertained almost continuously on these floating vacations.

Each year, at least ten new ships are built to accommodate the growing popularity of cruising. On cruises, the voyage itself is the vacation.

Answer the questions about the reading.

1. The first *transatlantic* voyage took place in the _____.

2. Use context clues to figure out what *transatlantic* in paragraph 2 means. Circle the correct definition below.

     across the United States

     going up into space

     crossing the Atlantic Ocean

     across the Pacific Ocean

3. The first cruise ships were much smaller and less comfortable than cruise ships built today. *True* or *false*? _____

4. The *Princess Victoria Luise* was the first cruise ship. What happened to it?

_____

_____

5. The word *grounded* in paragraph 3 means ___.

    a. driven onto the shore   **b.** forced to live underground

    c. having dug a hole   **d.** pounded into a fine powder

6. Number the events surrounding the *Titanic* in the correct order.

   ___ The *Titanic* sank the next day.

   ___ The *Titanic* was sailing across the Atlantic Ocean.

   ___ The *Titanic* hit an iceberg.

   ___ The *Titanic* set sail in spring of 1912.

7. Why did the author write this passage? ___

    a. to entertain   **b.** to persuade

    c. to share a historical event   **d.** to inform

8. Why did the cruise ship industry become less popular during the 1960s?

_____

9. About how many ships are being built each year to keep up with the cruise industry? _____

10. Have you ever gone on a cruise? Would you like to go on one someday? Why or why not?

_____

_____

Hot Air Helps

They may be an impractical way to travel, but hot-air balloons combine wind and scientific principles to create a fun and uplifting way to get around. Hot-air balloons were invented in France around 1783, when two French papermakers discovered that hot air made a fabric bag rise. The first large hot-air balloons held no passengers. After sending up all kinds of small animals, the first manned hot-air balloon voyage lasted 23 minutes. The balloon carried two men for 5.5 miles over Paris, France.

Since then, hot-air ballooning has grown to be a fun, recreational activity. There are about 7,500 hot air balloons licensed to operate in America. There are three main parts to these inflated giants. The large, colorful, balloon part, called the envelope, is composed of the same material as parachutes. This nylon or polyester is coated with a special material that makes the structure airtight, ensuring that the hot air stays in the balloon. The basket hangs below the envelope by a series of cables. Made of wicker, the basket is lightweight, strong, and flexible. Above the basket is the burner.

Scientists know that warm air rises because hot air is lighter than cool air. Based on this scientific principle, the air inside the envelope of the hot-air balloon must be hotter than the air around it. The pilot fires up the propane burner and heats the air enough to cause the balloon to rise. To do this, the pilot simply moves a control that opens up the valve on the propane tank. If the pilot keeps the valve open and the burner going, the balloon will continue to ascend.

At the top of every hot-air balloon is a "parachute," which is a control device attached to the basket by a cord. When the pilot wants the balloon to descend, he pulls this cord. This venting, or action that lets something escape, allows some of the hot air to slowly seep out of the balloon, which lowers the air temperature inside the envelope and causes it to sink toward the ground.

Knowledge of the wind conditions helps the pilot navigate the hot-air balloon left or right. The pilot can ascend or descend the balloon into the path of the wind, which increases as you go up. By changing altitude, or height, the pilot can better coax the balloon to move left or right.

The reason why hot-air balloons are unreliable forms of transportation is because wind is so changeable. That's why no one goes up in a balloon without someone in a car who will give the rider a way home from where they land. Those cars are called chase cars; they chase the hot-air balloons!

Answer the questions about the reading.

1. The three main parts of a hot-air balloon are ___.
    a. basket, weights, balloon   **b.** envelope, basket, burner
    c. basket, burner, parachute   **d.** burner, envelope, air

2. There are about _____ hot-air balloons licensed to operate in America.

3. Hot air is lighter than cool air. *True* or *false*? _____

4. Underline how the pilot lifts a hot-air balloon off the ground.
    The pilot heats the air in the envelope with a propane burner.
    The pilot fires up the engines.
    The pilot cools the air in the envelope.
    The pilot steps on the gas pedal and steers.

5. What happens if the pilot keeps the propane burner going?
_____

6. To move left or right in a hot-air balloon, the pilot must move up or down to find winds blowing in the desired direction. *True* or *false*? _____

7. On a separate sheet of paper, draw a simple diagram of a hot-air balloon. Label its three main parts.

8. Hot-air balloons come in all shapes and sizes. Draw and decorate your own hot-air balloon on another sheet of paper.

9. Pretend that you own a hot-air balloon company. Name your company and write a sentence that would entice people to take a short trip for fun.
_____

_____

10. Would you want to go up in a hot-air balloon? Why or why not?
_____

_____

Follow Directions, Please

Have you ever tried to put something together without reading the directions first? Following steps in the correct order can be the difference between success or failure. People who write directions make sure they are specific, clear, and in the correct order.

My sister makes the best baked apples in the microwave. Here are her directions:

> **1.** Wash an apple.
> **2.** Cut the apple into four wedges, making sure to remove the core.
> **3.** Place the wedges into a bowl and sprinkle with sugar and cinnamon.
> **4.** Cook in the microwave for four minutes.
> **5.** Make sure an adult is nearby when you remove the bowl because it will be very hot.
> **6.** Let the apple cool, and enjoy.

Now it's your turn. Think of something you can do that you could easily teach a friend to do, too. Write the steps below in the correct order.

_____

_____

_____

_____

_____

_____

_____

That Happened When?

Knowing the order of events helps you understand a story better. If authors wrote the happenings out of order, then the story would be very difficult to follow. But sometimes the author has to go back in time, or create a flashback, to explain something. He or she will use certain techniques to help the reader understand and follow what is happening.

Read the following paragraph. The author prepares the character to remember something that happened when she was in first grade.

Marta couldn't believe her mother was letting her get a dog. They talked about it for weeks and decided to go to the animal shelter in their town. As Marta walked through the front door of the shelter, she could hear the barks and howls of the dogs that were inside. She was worried about narrowing her choice to just one. She felt sad for all of them, but after she met the people who worked there, she knew that the dogs were loved and cared for. As she and her mother walked along the cages, she passed all kinds of dogs. They looked at almost every dog. Then Marta saw Jake. She fell in love with him immediately. She stepped back and remembered Toby. Toby was the husky she had when she was in the first grade.

Write your own ending to this story by writing a flashback that explains what Marta remembers about Toby.

_____

_____

_____

_____

_____

_____

_____

_____

Elephants Never Forget

One day, while Iain Douglas-Hamilton was watching a herd of African elephants feeding, the oldest female charged the truck he was driving. She ran toward the truck and hooked her tusks in the truck's tailgate. As he accelerated to escape harm's way, the elephant flipped her tusks upward. The truck was almost tossed upside down. The crew riding inside was almost thrown out. At that moment they were filming a documentary; the film crew and Douglas-Hamilton did not expect that kind of hostile behavior from the elephant.

According to Douglas-Hamilton, who has been watching elephants for many years, elephants don't forget. He says that older elephants living in the Tsavo National Park remember when thousands of elephants were killed by poachers in the 1970s and 1980s. These people trespassed on land that was protected in the park, which is the largest national park in Kenya, Africa. They killed the elephants for their ivory tusks, which were sold and made into jewelry, statues, and other items. Douglas-Hamilton is one scientist who believes that the elephants have not forgotten that terrible time in their history. He says that is why the elephant matriarch, or oldest female in the herd, charged at his film crew that afternoon.

In his journal, Douglas-Hamilton documented what happened. He wrote that after the elephant charged and attacked his truck, she pulled away with her head held high. He wrote that she looked as if she were celebrating a great victory before she ran back into the thick bush. The scientist believes that the matriarch was acting out her aggression toward humans that stems from what happened to her ancestors more than 30 years ago. He wrote in his journal that she appeared to attack because they were humans, and she felt that she had to protect her family.

In his journal, Douglas-Hamilton wrote that the elephants had not forgotten. The slaughter of elephants years ago is a well-documented fact. The attack on his truck was a fact, too, and can be proven because the crew captured it on film. But Douglas-Hamilton's ideas and theories about why the older elephant charged are merely speculation. He combines what he knows about the history of the African elephants with his experiences in the field. That is the first step in forming a hypothesis, or explanation.

Do elephants really remember? Some scientists will say no. But if you ask Iain Douglas-Hamilton, he will agree, based on what happened to him one afternoon in the Tsavo National Park in Kenya, Africa.

Answer the questions about the reading.

1. What does Iain Douglas-Hamilton do? ____
   a. He writes stories about elephants.
   b. He is a photographer.
   c. He is a scientist who studies elephants.
   d. He travels around the world taking pictures of animals.

2. Douglas-Hamilton and his crew were filming a _____ when their truck was attacked by an elephant.

3. Use context clues to determine what the word *poacher* in paragraph 2 means. Place a check next to all the clues that help you.
   a. ____ They went on land they weren't allowed to be on.
   b. ____ They protected elephants.
   c. ____ They killed many elephants.
   d. ____ They sold the elephants' ivory tusks.

4. Douglas-Hamilton believes that elephants today remember what happened to their ancestors in the 1970s and 1980s. *True* or *false*? _____

5. Why do you think Douglas-Hamilton keeps a journal?
   _____

6. How do we know that the attack on Douglas-Hamilton's truck really happened? ____
   a. He says it did.   **b.** He is making a documentary.
   c. His film crew captured the event on camera.   **d.** Someone nearby saw what happened.

7. A synonym for *hypothesis* is _____.

8. Number the steps that Douglas-Hamilton takes to form a hypothesis about elephants.
   ____ He studies elephants for a long time.
   ____ He records everything he sees and experiences.
   ____ He combines everything that he knows to explain something.
   ____ He reads as much as he can about elephants.

9. A *speculation* is something that someone ____.
   a. knows for a fact is true   **b.** believes to be true
   c. understands and can talk about   **d.** can't see but knows is there

99

The Kennedy Brothers

It was 1962. Russia was trying to install nuclear missiles in Cuba. President John F. Kennedy learned this after American military jets discovered the missiles during a reconnaissance flight. During one of these flights, whose purpose was to search for and gather military information, many photographs were taken. These pictures proved that missiles were being transported and stored in Cuba. The president had a big decision to make. The wrong choice could have started a war.

President Kennedy and his younger brother, Robert, were close. They shared the same hopes and dreams for all the American people. Robert Kennedy would be a lawyer, campaign manager, senator, and attorney general in his lifetime. He was the seventh of nine children and claimed to have learned more about politics and the world at his family's dinner table than at law school. With his help, John was elected the thirty-fifth President of the United States in 1960.

When John F. Kennedy became president, one of the first things he did was appoint his brother to be the U.S. Attorney General. Robert was his brother's closest advisor and sounding board. John sought and valued his brother's opinion. Working together in the White House, the brothers relied on each other. John and Robert would sit for hours, discussing issues and how they could be resolved. Their belief that problems could be solved in nonviolent ways helped prevent a war during the Cuban Missile Crisis. The Kennedy brothers discussed the dire situation.

After talking with his brother, President Kennedy decided to blockade, or stop, the transportation of all weapons on their way to Cuba. By using this strategy, Kennedy was then able to negotiate with leaders from the Soviet Union to have the missiles removed. This is one example of the Kennedy brothers' cooperation to solve problems that affected many people.

President Kennedy was in office for a little more than 1,000 days when he was assassinated in Dallas, Texas, on November 22, 1963. That event changed Robert's life. He left his job at the White House and ran for the U.S. Senate. He was elected in New York in 1965 and worked to help poor children and their families, and students with disabilities. His strong sense of responsibility drove him to follow in his brother's footsteps. In March 1968, Robert announced that he would run for president. But, after less than three months of campaigning, Robert was shot. He died on June 5, 1968. He was 42 years old.

Robert and John Kennedy, were raised to fight for the things they believed in. They relied on each other and made many great improvements that affected the lives of millions of Americans.

Answer the questions about the reading.

1. John and Robert Kennedy had a strong and close relationship. *True* or *false*? _____

2. Circle the idiom in this sentence from the reading: *His strong sense of responsibility drove him to decide to follow in his brother's footsteps.*

3. The idiom above means: _____

_____.

4. The Cuban Missile Crisis took place in _____.

   1958   1962   1963   1968

5. The reading states that Robert believed that he learned more about politics and the world at his family's dinner table. Make an inference about what life may have been like when John and Robert were young boys. _____

_____

6. Robert was his brother's *sounding board*. What does that mean? ____
   a. It means that John never asked Robert his thoughts on anything.
   b. It means that John and Robert had the same opinions about everything.
   c. It means that John respected Robert's opinions and asked him what he thought about things.
   d. It means that the brothers were close and talked all the time.

7. Circle the words in the word bank that describe what kind of person Robert Kennedy was.

    smart   compassionate   selfish   responsible   uncaring   determined

8. Circle the sentence in the reading that states whether Robert Kennedy ever ran for President.

9. Place a check next to each nonviolent solution to a problem.
   a. ____ discussing solutions
   b. ____ asking other people for their opinions
   c. ____ fighting and sending armies to force something to change
   d. ____ putting a blockade on goods or services

10. Why do you think it is important for leaders like President John Kennedy to have someone they trust to talk to?

_____

_____

It's All About Me

Things happen to us every day. We meet new people. We see strange and interesting stuff. We hear our friends and family make funny comments. To help them remember all the things they see, do, and hear, many writers like to keep a diary, or a daily journal.

Journaling is an easy thing to do. Get a plain notebook and decorate it with pictures, photographs, and anything that helps make it all about *you*. Start by introducing yourself on page one. Write everything about yourself that you can think of. Mention your family and friends, your home, your school, and the things you like to do.

Some people draw pictures and doodles, and some write in different colored inks. Find your style, and know that journaling every day will not only help improve your writing skills, but it might help you think about ways to solve problems in your life.

So get started! Design a cover for your journal. Think of things you like. Use your favorite colors. Be creative. Then name your journal. Write it on the cover below.

Write Right Now

Now that you have designed the perfect journal, here are the rules for journal writing: There are no rules! Journals are for writing whatever you want. They can be shared or kept private. It's up to you. You might even want to place a little note on the front cover that asks people not to look, if that's what you want.

Right now, spend a few minutes looking around you. Notice the things that are happening. Notice who is there. Watch what they're doing. Then write on the lines below.

Try to write for a few minutes without stopping. Describe what you saw. As you write, think about how these things make you feel. Do they remind you of a time when you and a friend did the same thing? Does what you see make you think of something you did when you were younger?

Cows Don't Get Mad

Sometimes the word *mad* means "angry" and sometimes it means "crazy." But when describing a disease that affects cows, *mad* means neither one.

Mad cow disease doesn't make cows angry or crazy. It makes them very sick. Also called *bovine spongiform encephalopathy* (pronounced BOH-vine SPUHN-jih-form ehn-seh-fah-LAH-puh-thee), or BSE, the disease affects the brains and central nervous system of cows. This disease is degenerative, which means that it causes a gradual worsening in the cow's condition. It damages brain tissue and may make the animal act nervous or violent. One way to tell if a cow is sick with mad cow disease is that it will have trouble walking. The cow may also act strangely.

Scientists are not really sure how cows get sick with this disease. They know it cannot be transmitted from one cow to another, but they think it may be spread in cattle feed made from cows that were infected with mad cow disease. So in 1997, the U.S. Food and Drug Administration, or FDA, banned the use of protein from animals in the manufacture of cattle feed. Feed makers are no longer allowed to add parts from cows and other animals to food that will nourish other cows. This rule helps to protect healthy cows from infection.

By the end of 2005, about 200 people throughout the world contracted a human form of mad cow disease. Called variant Creutzfeldt-Jakob disease, or vCJD, the condition causes infected people to gradually lose control of their physical and mental abilities. Scientists believe that people who have vCJD contracted it from eating beef products that came from cows infected with mad cow disease.

On a positive note, neither mad cow disease nor vCJD is contagious. People cannot catch mad cow disease just by being around infected cows. People also cannot catch vCJD from other people who have it. Scientists have also discovered that people cannot contract the disease by drinking milk that came from a sick cow.

The U.S. Food and Drug Administration and Department of Agriculture are working to protect both people and cows from the disease. Besides the ban on using cow parts to make cow feed, manufacturers are not allowed to use some cow parts, such as the brain and spinal cord, from cows older than 30 months. They are also not allowed to use them in makeup, lotions, and other cosmetics.

Answer the questions about the reading.

1. In this reading, the author uses the word *mad*, an example of a multiple-meaning word. Which sentence is an example of the first definition mentioned in the reading? ____

a. The crowd had a mad time at the celebration.

b. Not being allowed to go on the trip made the boy mad.

c. "This itchy spot on my arm is driving me mad," said Jody.

d. She ran like mad to catch the bus.

2. Another multiple-meaning word is *feed*. Place a check next to the two meanings for the word *feed* that are used in the reading.

a. ____ food for farm animals

b. ____ to push slowly into a machine

c. ____ to give cues to an actor

d. ____ to serve as food

3. Mad cow disease makes cows very sick and affects the way they behave. *True* or *false*?

_____

4. Scientists think that cows contract mad cow disease from infected feed that they eat. That discovery caused something important to happen. What was this effect? ____

a. Cows were cured of mad cow disease.

b. The FDA made a new rule that banned companies from using cow parts in their feed.

c. The U.S. Department of Agriculture began making its own feed for cows.

d. The United States started purchasing animal feed from other countries.

5. Underline the sentence in the reading that states what the new rule accomplishes.

6. By the end of 2005, how many people were infected with vCJD? _____

7. People can get mad cow disease by drinking milk from infected cows. *True* or *false*?

_____

8. The word *contagious* in paragraph 5 means ____.

a. able to spread from one person or animal to another   **b.** safe and contained

c. not easily spread or transmitted   **d.** causing difficulty in breathing

9. An antonym for the word *ban* in paragraph 6 is ____.

a. forbid   **b.** spend   **c.** show up   **d.** allow

MP3 and Me

Years ago, the only way to listen to your favorite band whenever you wanted to was to slip a black, vinyl record out of its cover and play it on a record player. Through the years, people have taken their tunes with them in the form of 8-track tapes, cassette tapes, and CDs. Now, you can carry thousands of your favorite songs on a personal music player.

It sings. It swings. It holds hours and hours of music and plays your favorite tunes whenever you want to hear them. Small enough to fit in the palm of your hand, today's digital audio players have taken listening to music to a higher level. Introduced in 1997 by the Moving Pictures Expert Group (MPEG), the first MPEG Audio Player III, or MP3, player started a technological craze that innovated the way we listen to music. That year, the new portable music players were much bigger and held less music than the new generation of players sold in stores today.

This is how they work. Songs that are stored on CDs are in a digital format, which is a form readable by computers. One CD can store up to about 74 minutes of music. The songs are uncompressed, which means that they have not been altered to fit into a smaller amount of space. So, for example, one three-minute song requires about 32 million bytes, or units, on a CD. Using a special system that compresses, or squeezes together, audio files, an MP3 player takes that same three-minute song and squashes it so that it takes up less memory space, all without damaging the quality of the sound.

Using this compression method, an MP3 player with 1,000 megabytes of storage space can hold about 240 songs. This compression method makes music much easier to store and retrieve whenever you want to. In fact, in 2008, the iPod, a digital music player manufactured by Apple Inc., could hold up to 2,000 songs.

As an owner of an MP3 player, you can do many amazing things. You can easily download any song from a CD or your computer and play it whenever you want. You can record your own music and convert, or change, it into an audio file that can be stored on your player. You can also store hundreds of songs and listen to them easily. For many music lovers, the MP3 player is a technological advancement that they can't live without.

Answer the questions about the reading.

1. The word *uncompressed* in paragraph 3 means _____.
   a. pressed into a smaller amount of space
   b. flattened by pressure
   c. not altered to fit into a smaller amount of space
   d. difficult or unable to understand

2. Which company introduced the first MP3 player in 1997? _____

Complete the chart below, explaining how an MP3 player works:

An MP3 player **3.** _____ songs from a CD.

4. They are _____ on an MP3 player, which can hold a lot of songs.

5. Turn on your MP3 player and _____.

6. CDs store about _____ minutes of music.

7. Some new digital music players can store up to _____ songs.

8. What can an MP3 player **not** do? _____
   a. download music from your computer
   b. store hundred of songs
   c. make up songs and record them
   d. allow you to take music with you, wherever you go

9. The word *convert* in paragraph 5 means _____.
   a. change
   b. exchange for something of lesser value
   c. shoot and score a goal
   d. person who changes his or her mind about something

10. What kind of music do you like to listen to? Do you listen to it on an MP3 player?

_____

_____

_____

How the Writer Hooks the Reader

Those who love to read also love to read good writing. Good authors know that word choice is important, especially if they want their readers to keep reading. To do that, authors spend a lot of time choosing their words.

Read this sentence: *The small cat looked out the window at the bird.*

With just a few careful word substitutions, this sentence can become: *The scrawny cat gazed longingly out the window at the irritating bird.*

The meaning of the sentence hasn't changed, but the reader's mental image of the cat has. That is because the author replaced some of the words with more interesting choices and added an adverb and an adjective to help describe what was happening.

Rewrite the following sentences, making word choice a priority. Good luck. Or, instead, superior fortuity!

1. She watched the scary movie with her friends.

_____

_____

2. "I have a bad headache," said my mother.

_____

_____

3. The silly joke made everyone laugh hard.

_____

_____

4. My brother likes to eat crackers and sip milk when he watches television.

_____

_____

5. The day we went to see the Grand Canyon, it rained so hard that the road flooded.

_____

_____

Sometimes Less Is More

When an author adds more interesting words to sentences, the story comes alive for the reader. This technique helps transform the words on a page into captivating mental images. Colorful word choices that add more details seem like always a good thing. But, sometimes, more is not necessarily better. Sometimes more is too much.

Here is an example: *The frustrated boy wrestled and struggled with the windswept umbrella as the sky began to pour furiously.*

This sentence, while it certainly does describe a vivid scene, is difficult to read. This sentence is a good example of one that could be just as descriptive with fewer words: *The frustrated boy struggled with the windswept umbrella as the sky began to pour.*

The following sentences may be difficult to read. Read each one and decide if it sounds correct. If it doesn't, take out a word or two. Perhaps change one or two words. But rewrite it to make it simpler without changing its meaning.

1. The enthusiastic child jumped crazily up and down in his paved driveway when he saw his devoted father carefully steer the car down the street.

_____

_____

2. The ripe, shiny apples would be cut into pieces and made into a delicious pie.

_____

3. My large dog leaps onto the comfortable sofa every time we leave the house.

_____

4. The brave firefighter marched courageously into the burning building.

_____

5. The black cat purred loudly as its affectionate owner slowly brushed its soft, sleek fur.

_____

On the Surface

It is lightweight, colorful, and easy to control. It can float just about anywhere. It doesn't even frighten ducks. In a time when bigger and louder always seems to be better, the kayak is a smaller and quieter alternative to enjoying the great outdoors.

First used by the Inuit, a tribe of people who lived in the Arctic, the first kayak was made from sealskins and wooden frames. There was a small hole in the middle of the top of the boat where the paddler sat. Back then, kayaks were used mostly for hunting.

The material used to build kayaks has changed. Sealskins were replaced by fabric, though wooden frames were still used until the 1950s. During that decade, fiberglass was invented. Kayaks were then constructed from this lightweight material, which is made from fine glass fibers and used to insulate, reinforce, and make things stronger. By 1984, kayaks were manufactured out of plastic. Like fiberglass, plastic also makes kayaks lightweight, sturdy, and able to move freely in the water.

Kayaking has become a popular sport for people who are interested in exploring rivers and streams, and fishing and photography. Most of the kayaks sold today are to recreational kayakers. These boats have a larger cockpit, or opening, so that the paddler can get in and out more easily. Recreational kayaks are also built to be more stable, or steady, on the water. They are usually less than 12 feet long and have room to store a few things in front and behind the person seated in the center.

Kayaks can go where larger boats and motorboats cannot. In fact, a kayak can slip quietly through the water without disturbing wildlife. Even the paddles are designed to propel the boat easily and silently in shallow water. The kayak sits low in the water. Because of its flat bottom, about six inches of water is just enough to make it float. While nestled inside a kayak, the paddler can easily reach over the edge of the boat and touch the water.

Kayaking has grown in popularity and now meets the needs of many people interested in the sport. There are boats for touring, racing, playing, and competing. In 1936, kayaking was even introduced as an Olympic sport.

Answer the questions about the reading.

1. The word *kayak* is a palindrome. That means it is spelled the same way forward and backward. Circle the words in the word bank that are palindromes.

Mom   David   civic   motor   radar   level   garden   madam

2. Fiberglass is a ____
   a. manmade material that is weak and cannot get wet.
   b. lightweight material made from fine glass fibers.
   c. heavy plastic material that does not float on the water.
   d. type of plastic that is difficult to make and use.

3. Fiberglass was invented in the _____.

4. Most of the kayaks sold today are for people who ____. Place a check next to all that apply.
   a. ____ want to race
   b. ____ want to photograph wildlife
   c. ____ want to get some exercise while enjoying nature
   d. ____ are interested in learning stunts and tricks

5. *Stable* is a multiple-meaning word. Which defintion applies to its use in the reading? ____
   a. a building where horses and cows live
   b. permanent
   c. a group of entertainers who share the same management or agent
   d. not easily tipped

6. Place a check next to the statments that are true.
   a. ____ Kayaks can go where larger boats cannot.
   b. ____ Recreational kayaks are easily tipped over in the water.
   c. ____ Kayaking is becoming a popular recreational sport.

7. A kayak's paddle is designed to move the boat through the water both
   _____ and _____.

8. The first time kayakers competed in the Olympics was in _____.

9. The first kayaks were used mostly for _____.
   recreation   hunting   racing   competing

Poetry and Motion

Motion Detectors

I slide my soccer shoes on,
And I become a superstar.
Sailing, leaping, racing across the field of green.
I am graceful and strong.
I am running with the wind.
I am unstoppable and able to kick and turn.
My shoes are motion detectors,
They follow the ball.
I do not choose where I run.
My shoes choose for me.

Ballet Shoes

Feet pointed, knees bent, arms outstretched,
My ballet shoes fit me better than anyone can know.
They take me places near and far,
They take me wherever I want to go.
The music begins and my feet wake up,
Ballet shoes come alive and make my toes smile.
I am in motion. A great graceful, gliding spin.
Full of energy, happiness, and style.

Old Sneakers

Before they were old, they were new.
I carefully stepped around puddles and mud.
I tried to keep them clean. I tried to keep them perfect.
Before I knew it, they were less than spotless.
They turned into a comfortable haven for my feet to live in.
They longed to slosh through water on the pond's edge.
They begged for me to stamp in rainy gutters.
Before they were old, they were new,
And then they became my friends.

Answer the questions about the poems.

1. What themes are common to all three poems? _____

_____

2. In "Motion Detectors," the root word of *unstoppable* is *stop*. Think about the word's prefix and suffix, and then underline the definition.

    Unstoppable means "able to stop something."

    Unstoppable means "unable to be stopped."

    Unstoppable means "taking the time to stop something."

    Unstoppable means "easily stoppable."

3. In the first poem, to what is the poet comparing her soccer shoes? _____

Circle the line in the poem that explains the metaphor.

4. What do you think the first line in "Ballet Shoes" describes? _____

_____

5. The phrase "great graceful, gliding" is an alliteration, which means that the beginning sounds are repeated. Reread "Ballet Shoes" and think of an alliteration about dancing or movement.

_____

6. The author of "Old Sneakers" repeated a line in the poem. Underline both instances.

7. Place a check next to the sentences below from "Old Sneakers" that are examples of personification.

    a. _____ Before I knew it, they were less than spotless.

    b. _____ They longed to slosh through water on the pond's edge.

    c. _____ They begged for me to stamp in rainy gutters.

    d. _____ And then they became my friends.

8. The author wrote in "Old Sneakers" that he or she stepped around puddles and mud to try to keep the new sneakers clean. *True* or *false*? _____

9. Think about your favorite pair of shoes. Write two lines describing the things they help you do.

_____

_____

10. Now describe how they make you feel.

_____

_____

One Out of Many

When people think of the United States of America, they may think of the red, white, and blue flag, the bald eagle, and Uncle Sam. All three are familiar icons, or symbols, of America. But there is one more emblem that represents what this country stands for. That symbol is the Great Seal.

On the Great Seal of the United States is an American bald eagle holding a ribbon in its mouth. On the ribbon are the words *E pluribus unum*, which mean "one out of many." This describes how one nation rises out of many colonies. The eagle is also pictured clutching a bundle of 13 arrows in one of its sharp talons and an olive branch in the other. The arrows represent the original colonies and how real the threat of war is. The olive branch stands for the power of peace. Across its chest is a shield with 13 stripes. According to Charles Thomson, the man who designed the Great Seal in 1782, the stripes symbolized the union between the states and the new government. He also designed a crest above the eagle's head, which contains a constellation of 13 stars.

Thomson served as the Secretary of the Continental Congress for 15 years. His picture can be seen on the back of the two-dollar bill in the engraving of the Declaration of Independence. Thomson is standing to the right of John Hancock. As he designed the Great Seal, Thomson made a symbol that stood for the ideals of America.

The other side of the seal shows an unfinished pyramid with an eye above it. Everything on the Great Seal was chosen because of its meaning. Thomson chose the pyramid because it symbolizes strength and something that will last forever. Along the base of the pyramid are the Roman numerals MDCCLXXVI. These numerals stand for 1776, the year America's Founding Fathers signed the Declaration of Independence. The eye above the pyramid signifies that the colonies were watched over and protected. The mottos, or phrases, on the pyramid side of the seal stand for the same idea.

Thomson wished that the Great Seal would give hope to the country. He designed both sides of the icon to show Americans that they were strong and could endure anything. Because America was new when the seal was created, it signifies the country's beginning and the promise that it and its people would grow and prosper. Like the U.S. flag, American bald eagle, and Uncle Sam, the Great Seal of the United States of America represents this country.

Answer the questions about the reading.

1. Another word for an *icon* is _____.

    sign   advertisement   symbol   cartoon

2. Charles Thomson designed the Great Seal in _____.

3. The eagle on the seal is holding 13 arrows. It has 13 stripes across its chest. There are 13 stars above its head. What does the number 13 symbolize? _____
    a. The number of years the colonists lived in America.
    b. The number of original colonies in America.
    c. The number of times America was at war.
    d. The number of Presidents who served the country.

4. If you wanted to see what Charles Thomson looked like, where could you find a picture of him?
_____

5. Everything on the Great Seal was chosen because of its meaning. *True* or *false*?
_____

6. In what year did America's Founding Fathers sign the Declaration of Independence?
_____

    1796   1976   1725   1776

7. A synonym for the word *motto* in paragraph 4 is _____.
    song   poem   phrase   book

8. Thomson created the Great Seal to give _____ to Americans.

9. His designs showed Americans that they were _____.
    a. strong and could endure anything   **b.** weak and needed help
    c. good at dealing with problems   **d.** ready to move to another part of the country

10. Circle the names of three other American icons mentioned in the reading.

Buzz! Crackle! Slurp!

"**Buzz**, buzz," said the bee.

My cereal went **crackle**, crackle, **pop**.

Emily **slurped** her milkshake through a straw.
These sentences have one thing in common. They each contain a word or words that sound like the thing they name or the sounds they make. This literary device is called *onomatopoeia*.

Onomatopoeia, pronounced on-uh-maht-uh-PEE-uh, is derived from Greek words that mean "name making." Onomatopoeia are words that look like the sound they make when you say them. Writers use onomatopoeia to convey the sounds of the things they are writing about. Using *onomatopoeia* makes reading more fun. And just saying *onomatopoeia* is fun, too!

Here are a few examples of onomatopoeia: *swish, arf, brrr, honk, meow,* and *quack*. In the word box, write as many examples of onomatopoeia that you can think of:

Now use some of those words to write sentences. Feel free to use more than one in each sentence!

Marvelous Comic Strips

Comic strips are fun to read. They are colorful, action-packed, and filled with words that look like the sounds they make. You remember what those words are called, right? People who write comic books use onomatopoeia all the time. But comic strips are a good way to sharpen your comprehension skills. As you read, the space between each comic panel is a place where your imagination can kick in. You can make inferences, draw conclusions, and think about how the characters are portrayed.

In a newspaper, look at some examples of comic strips. See what they have in common. Then make up your own comic strip below. Your characters can be animals, people, superheroes, or even your friends. Use some words from page 116 to enhance your comic. Then color it and share it with a friend.

The Thrill of It All

Some people go to amusement parks for the food. Some go for the entertainment. Some even go to throw ping-pong balls into fishbowls to win small prizes. But there's one group of people who visit amusement parks for one reason and one reason only: to scream.

These are people who like to go fast. They like to feel the wind in their hair as they plummet down a steep track. They like to hear the sounds of their own screams as they realize they are higher than they've ever been and are going faster than they've ever gone. These are the people who go to amusement parks to ride the roller coaster.

Roller coasters have come a long way since their earliest beginnings in the 1600s. Evidence of the very first roller coaster can be found in Russia. People sat on large blocks of ice covered with straw or fur as they were pulled up and down hills. In those days, sand was scattered at the bottom of the hills. The friction created as the ice block rode over the sand slowed the ride down. Over time, ice blocks were replaced by wooden sleds and tracks. Then, in 1875, Coney Island in New York was created. This was America's first amusement park.

In 1955, Disneyland, America's most famous and first theme amusement park, was opened in California. Roller coasters had always been built out of wood. But in 1959, the first tubular steel coaster was built at Disneyland. It had loops, a corkscrew track, and was more stable and safer than wooden coasters. True thrill-seekers prefer steel roller coasters because they are taller and faster. They also have more loops, longer drops, and steeper hills. So for the true scream-seeking coaster lover, Disneyland's Matterhorn was the beginning of a dream come true.

Roller coasters can go as fast as 60 miles an hour without an engine. The coaster is pulled to the top of a hill when the ride starts and begins its descent down the first hill of the ride. The smooth rail and wheels that steer, balance, and slow it down help keep the ride going. After that first big push, the coaster continues on its journey, careening up and down, until it comes to a stop. For many roller coaster riders, life doesn't get any better than this.

Answer the questions about the reading.

1. The first roller coaster was created during the _____.

2. Friction is created when one thing rubs across something else. What did the Russians use to create friction in their early roller coasters? _____
   a. ice blocks and blankets
   b. hay and ice blocks
   c. ice blocks and sand
   d. sand and blankets

3. Friction made the roller coasters go faster. *True* or *false*? _____

4. The word *stable* is a multiple-meaning word. Which definition applies to its use in the reading? _____
   a. no change in a sick person's condition
   b. barn
   c. sturdy and reliable
   d. a group of animals

5. Number the events from the reading in the correct order.
   _____ The Matterhorn, the first tubular steel coaster, was built at Disneyland.
   _____ Coney Island opened.
   _____ Disneyland was created and opened to the public.
   _____ The Russians invented the roller coaster.

6. Why do people who love roller coasters tend to like steel roller coasters more than wooden ones? _____

7. Roller coasters can go as fast as _____ miles per hour.

8. With just one good push, a roller coaster can continue its ride, thanks to the steep hills and smooth rails. *True* or *false*? _____

9. Using context clues, what do you think the word *careening* in the last paragraph means? _____
   a. moving side to side while going very fast
   b. tipping over
   c. moving slowly and carefully on a track
   d. coming to a slow and careful stop

10. If you were designing a roller coaster, what three important things would you make sure to include?

_____

_____

Look! Up in the Sky!

They look light and fluffy. They float above your head like puffs of cotton, moving slowly across the sky. Clouds are more than what they seem to be. Here you will learn about what clouds are made of, why they aren't always white, and how they form.

Clouds begin as tiny droplets of water. These droplets can float in the air because they are so small and almost weightless. But when these droplets are close to the ground, they exist in the form of an invisible gas called water vapor. If this air warms and, thus, rises, it moves up into a cooler part of the air that surrounds earth. This cool air is unable to hold as much water vapor as warm air.

Some of these water vapor droplets cool and they condense, or become a liquid or solid. They attach themselves to tiny pieces of dust that are always floating around in the sky. When billions of these congregate, a cloud is born. It may seem hard to believe that billions of droplets of water and dust could float, but they do, as long as the air in the cloud is warmer than the air around it.

Whether a cloud is white or gray depends on many things. As you may know, the sun's light is composed of all the colors of the rainbow, and when those colors unite, the light appears white. Clouds are white because they reflect all the colors from the sun. Clouds turn gray, however, when they become so thick or are floating so high that the light above them cannot get through. Some clouds also look gray if they are in the shadow of other clouds nearby.

Scientists classify clouds in different ways, such as high, middle, and low clouds. The most common type of high cloud is the cirrus cloud. Cirrus clouds look thin and wispy. They are usually white and can be seen during pleasant weather. Middle clouds are usually gray and cover the entire sky. They form ahead of storms and bring rain or snow. Low clouds, such as stratus clouds, look more like thick, gray fog in the sky and tend to bring precipitation, too.

The white, puffy clouds in which you may see shapes of animals and other things are cumulus clouds. They seem to float effortlessly across the sky. It is up into these low clouds that you might lie on your back on sunny warm days and wonder.

Answer the questions about the reading.

1. Place a check next to each phrase that describes what the author wants you to learn in the reading:

    a. ____ why clouds aren't always white   **b.** ____ what clouds are made of

    c. ____ why clouds sometimes look like animals and things   **d.** ____ how clouds form

2. Clouds are composed of tiny droplets of _____.

3. Warm air rises. *True* or *false*? _____

4. Number the steps of cloud formation in the correct order.

    ____ The water vapor droplets become liquid.

    ____ Warm air and the water vapor in it rise.

    ____ The condensed droplets attach themselves to dust particles.

    ____ The warm air and water vapor cool down.

5. A cloud is composed of billions of water droplets and dust particles. *True* or *false*?

    _____

6. Can you infer from this reading that if the air in a cloud becomes cooler than the air around it, it will sink to earth? _____ Circle the sentence that is your clue.

7. The most common type of high cloud is the _____.

8. Draw a diagram of the sky. Place high, middle, and low clouds in your diagram, making sure they match the description in the selection. Label the cirrus, stratus, and storm cumulus clouds.

Signed, Sealed, Stamped, and Delivered

The U.S. Postal Service, or USPS, issued a set of 15 new stamps during National Stamp Collecting month in October of 2004. The stamps showed 15 different clouds and included cirrus, stratus, cumulus, and tornado clouds.

The cloud stamps were issued at the Blue Hill Meteorological Observatory near Boston, Massachusetts, where meteorologists first began recording the weather in 1885. According to USPS officials, the new stamps were released to encourage people to think about the science of weather.

Consider your favorite topic in science or social studies. Is it maps? The oceans? Animals? Space travel? Choose one and design a set of six stamps below. Remember that they will appear on envelopes everywhere, so make sure they are accurate and colorful.

Extra! Extra! Read All About It

   Whenever the U.S. Postal Service releases a new set of stamps, their Public Relations department writes and sends out a press release to media such as newspapers and radio and television stations. This lets people know that new stamps are available. Many people collect stamps and like to purchase them as soon as they are issued. Other people just like to buy interesting stamps.

   A press release should contain information about who created the stamps, why they were created, and describe what they look like. The press release should be short, but contain enough information for people to learn everything they need to know about the new stamps.

   Write a press release for the stamps you designed on page 122. Make sure to include information about yourself, the creator of the stamps.

_____

_____

_____

_____

_____

_____

_____

_____

_____

_____

Global Warming and You

If you think kids can't change the world, just ask Alec Loorz. He and his friends live in Ventura, California. At their local movie theater they watched *An Inconvenient Truth*, the movie written by former U.S. Vice President Al Gore about global warming. After seeing the effects of global warming on earth, Alec founded Kids vs. Global Warming.

Kids vs. Global Warming is an organization that educates young people about the problems they may face in the future because of global warming. Alec says he thought that since people his age might be the most affected, they should all join together to do something about it.

According to scientists, global warming is an increase in the average temperature of earth's atmosphere. It causes the climate of earth to change and could result in flooding, drought, heat waves, and forest fires. Global warming could cause the polar ice caps and glaciers to melt and sea levels to rise. It is also expected to cause fluctuations, or changes, in temperature and rainfall, and result in stronger hurricanes and storms.

Alec and his friends are obviously concerned. They are cooperating to inform and encourage others to make changes and take action. Three projects they started are aimed at education. One is a local community activists' project that works to raise people's awareness of the rise in sea level off Ventura, their hometown. The members of Kids vs. Global Warming put up more than 120 signs around town to show how the sea level will look if it continues to rise. It is Alec's hope that people will see the signs and want to help.

Alec and his group also visit local schools, colleges, and environmental group meetings, where they give presentations about global warming. They talk about what global warming is and what young people can do to help prevent it and how. Thirdly, on Earth Day the group sets up interactive booths for kids and passes out information and suggestions.

Alec believes that global warming can be stopped. He believes that education is the first step, but also that everyone must pitch in right now. Some ideas that he shares include encouraging your parents to make sure your home is well insulated and weatherized. By properly insulating walls and ceilings, homeowners can save up to 25 percent of their home heating bill. That simple change also saves about 2,000 pounds of carbon dioxide a year. Alec also strongly advocates recycling paper and plastic products, planting trees, and buying products with less packaging.

Answer the questions about the reading.

1. Global warming is _____.
    a. a decrease in the temperature at the North and South poles
    b. an increase in the average temperature of Earth's atmosphere
    c. nothing anyone should be worried about
    d. when the air temperature becomes too warm to go outside

2. What sparked Alec's idea to start an organization about global warming? _____
_____

3. Alec founded Kids vs. Global Warming to educate other kids about the earth and their future.
True or *false*? _____

4. Make an inference about Alec. Describe the kind of person you think he must be.
_____

_____

5. The kids in Alec's group put up _____ signs in _____
to show people how the sea level is rising.

6. Place a check next to the sentences that describe things that Alec believes that people can do
right now to help the earth.
    a. _____ Insulate your home.   **b.** _____ Plant trees.
    c. _____ Drink more water.   **d.** _____ Recycle paper and plastic products.

7. Why do you think Alec thinks that people should buy products with less packaging?
_____

8. Using context clues, what do you think the word *advocates* in the last paragraph means? _____
    a. denies   **b.** argues against
    c. supports or recommends   **d.** pretends not to notice

9. How do you think Alec feels about what he and his friends are doing? Explain.
_____

10. Can you think of anything else you can do to help Alec and his organization? Describe your
suggestion.
_____

Wild Animal ER

Every day, all over the world, wild animals get sick or are injured. There are many things a person can do if they find such an animal in the wild.

According to the International Wildlife Rehabilitation Council, sometimes people who find wild animals want to take them home and care for them. That is not a good idea, though! First of all, laws may prohibit that. Each town and state has its own regulations about keeping a wild animal in your home or on your property. That is why there are wildlife rehabilitators and care centers. They have permission to detain, or hold onto, animals and treat them. Another important reason why people should not care for injured or lost animals is that sometimes these animals carry diseases that humans or their pets can contract. There are also diseases that wild animals can get from domestic pets.

Wildlife rehabilitators have the equipment and appropriate environment for caring for wild animals. These men and women are trained to deal with injuries and other conditions that an injured wild animal might have. Not all veterinarians have the skills to work with wild animals. After rehabilitators have administered medications, stabilized or supported an animal in shock, and tended to wounds, he or she may have to call a veterinarian. These professionals know which veterinarians they can call for advice.

Young animals who spend time with humans quickly learn not to fear them. When a wild animal is not afraid, it is in jeopardy of not surviving when it is released back in the wild. Rehabilitators know how to preserve the animal's wild nature while caring for its wounds.

The National Wildlife Rehabilitators Association recommends that adults approach injured animals slowly, and make sure they are really injured before getting too close. Animals that are bleeding or have obvious broken bones need help. Other signs include an absence of fear, uncoordinated movements, and an inability to run away. It is important to remember never to touch or get close to any wild animal. The best thing to do is let an adult know about your concerns for the animal.

If you need to transport a sick or injured wild animal to a care center, it is important to make sure the animal is in a quiet, dark spot. A box with a lid and air holes is a good idea. If the animal is very young, also make sure there is a source of heat nearby. Never give food to an injured wild animal. Once the nearest wildlife rehabilitation center has been contacted, follow the directions of the professional there. Sometimes they may recommend allowing the animal to rest overnight in the quiet spot because the stress of driving to and arriving at the clinic may have been more than the sick animal can handle.

Wildlife rehabilitators are trained and ready to help animals that cannot help themselves. Regular people can help them do their jobs by making sure to call.

Answer the questions about the reading.

1. A synonym for the word *regulations* in paragraph 2 is _____.

   speeches   articles   laws   tickets

2. According to wildlife rehabilitators, what is the effect on an injured young animal that loses its fear of humans?_____

3. Place a check next to the three reasons wildlife rehabilitators should be the only ones to take care of injured wild animals.

   a. _____ They are trained to deal with injuries wild animals might have.

   b. _____ They live near woods and can pick up animals quickly.

   c. _____ They know how to preserve the animal's fear of humans.

   d. _____ They have permission to keep and care for wild animals.

4. If a wild animal must be moved, it is important to transport it in a way that makes the animal feel safe. *True* or *false*? _____

5. Circle the sentences in the reading that give advice about your safety and what you should do instead of trying to help an injured animal yourself.

6. The National Wildlife Rehabilitators Association recommends that people approach injured animals _____.

   a. as quickly as possible   **b.** as slowly as possible

   c. without worrying about getting hurt   **d.** before checking to see if they are injured

7. An antonym of the word *stabilize* in paragraph 3 is _____.

   soothe   calm   nurture   aggravate

8. A wild animal that doesn't seem to be afraid of you, is moving in an uncoordinated way, or cannot run away from you may be _____.

9. Young animals need heat to survive. *True* or *false*? _____

10. What was the author's purpose in writing this passage?_____

   _____

Let's Get Organized

Graphic organizers are ways to take information we read and organize it. Teachers use these charts, diagrams, and maps to help their students better understand what they are reading. One example of a graphic organizer is a sequencing chart. As you read the following story, note the signal words *first, next,* and *finally* to help you complete the sequencing chart below it.

My father would take us fishing on summer Sunday mornings. My younger brothers and I would get dressed and put on our sneakers while he made small balls out of bread. The goldfish at Brookville Park really liked that bait!

When we arrived at the lake, the first thing we did was untangle our fishing rods. They would always somehow become tangled on the ride over. The next thing we did was bait our hooks. By the end of the summer, we wouldn't need to use even one of the bandages that my father kept in his wallet. As each one of us caught fish, my father would walk over proudly and help remove the fish. Finally, the fish would be gently placed back into the water.

I bet we caught some of those fish over and over again all summer long.

First

⬇

Next

⬇

Finally

Brainstorm Away

You can also use graphic organizers before you write. For example, sometimes an author will create an intricate word web to help organize thoughts and ideas. Here is an example of the author's word web for "Wild Animal ER" on page 126.

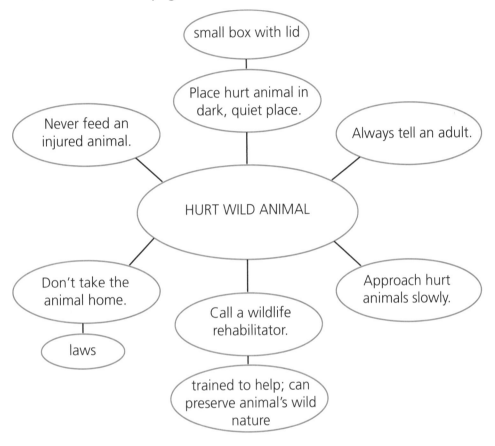

Think about an animal or story you like. Fill in the word web with as many ideas as you can. Remember that capturing ideas on paper can help you write later. Draw more ovals if you need to.

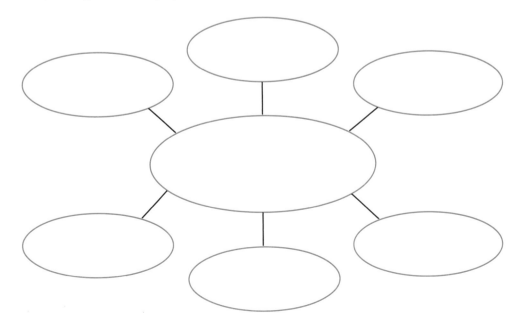

Beyond the Beach

If you think that standing on a beach in Florida is standing on one edge of America, you are wrong. The U.S. border reaches about 200 miles beyond its beaches. In that space, known as the Exclusive Economic Zone, there is much going on, including offshore oil drilling.

In every day of 2005, the United States produced about nine million barrels of crude oil and imported more than 13 million barrels from other countries. Each year the daily amount increases. Oil companies must spend a large amount of time looking for new places to acquire this oil. They also look for ways to improve the oil wells that are already in use.

Offshore oil rigs are installed on huge platforms in water and are used to drill for oil at the bottom of the ocean. Built to withstand ocean waves and storms, many of the oil platforms are taller than a skyscraper and float in very deep water. Made of steel, some of these structures are built on stilts that are anchored to the floor of the ocean. Some of them are floating and anchored to the ocean floor by thick, strong cables.

An oil rig, or drilling rig, houses equipment to make a hole in the ocean floor through which oil can be removed. The oil rig's job is to drill through the earth's crust and extract the oil. While removing the oil, the equipment also removes mud and sand.

Oil rig workers include welders, mechanics, electricians, engineers, and people who specialize in drilling and oil production. They all live and work together on the rig. Some rigs also have cooks, firefighters, computer technicians, radio operators, and pilots. Workers on offshore oil rigs usually stay on the platform for weeks at a time. They ride back and forth from shore on a boat or take a helicopter out to where the rig is.

Oil that is removed from underneath the ocean floor is called crude oil. Crude oil is a mixture of hydrocarbons that are produced when tiny plants and animals die and decay under layers of sand and mud. The crude oil that rigs are drilling for today has been under the ocean floor for millions of years.

When crude oil leaves an undersea well, it is usually mixed with gases and water. It is a caramel color with sand floating throughout it. Both the sand and water must be separated from the oil before it can leave the well. After that, it is taken by pipeline or tanker truck to be processed. After that, it is made into products that Americans use every day.

Answer the questions about the reading.

1. The U.S. border extends about _____ miles beyond land into the oceans.

2. One activity that happenes in the Exclusive Economic Zone is _____.

3. How much crude oil did the U.S. produce per day in 2005? ____
  a. 12 million barrels   **b.** 9 million barrels
  c. 2 million barrels   **d.** 19 million barrels

4. If the United States *imports* more than 13 million barrels of crude oil, that means it ____.
  a. sends goods out to other countries
  b. manufactures everything here in this country
  c. has no trade agreements with other countries
  d. brings in goods from other countries

5. Place a check next to two things that oil companies do every year.
  a. ____ They look for ways to improve the oil wells already in use.
  b. ____ They visit other countries to see how they produce oil.
  c. ____ They spend a lot of time looking for new places to acquire oil.
  d. ____ They try to think of ways to decrease their crude oil production.

6. How do offshore oil workers travel to and from work? _____

_____

7. Crude oil needs millions of years to develop. *True* or *false*?_____

8. Why do you think there are cooks, firefighters, and other kinds of workers on an offshore oil rig? Make an inference about why they are there. _____

_____

9. Place a check next to the conclusions you can draw about the offshore oil drilling industry.
  a. ____ Working on an offshore oil rig is probably hard work.
  b. ____ Men and women who work on oil rigs probably miss their families.
  c. ____ Offshore oil rigs are definitely fun places to work.
  d. ____ Working on an offshore oil rig can be dangerous work sometimes.

10. Would you like to spend time on an offshore oil rig? Why or why not?

_____

_____

Nicole's Edible Art Project

The air was getting cooler. The leaves were starting to fall from the trees that lined the streets. As Nicole walked from school to the small bakery shop her mother had just started, she buttoned her sweater and looked up into the blue sky. Her mother expected her to walk the three blocks from school, but she was always standing on the steps of her bakery shop, waving and waiting for her.

Nicole always told about her day as her mom poured a small glass of milk. After her snack, Nicole completed her homework and then was allowed to help in the bakery. Recently, her mother taught her how to frost and decorate cupcakes. Nicole loved to pipe, or squeeze, the colorful frosting through the pastry tube onto the tops of miniature cakes. She loved hearing the customers' reactions to her designs.

For as long as Nicole could remember, she loved art. She impressed her teachers every year with watercolor paintings and clay sculptures. She had won the school's art contest two years in a row and was working on this year's project when she began decorating cupcakes. Nicole had never considered baking to be an art form until now. She could see how her intricate and imaginative creations were inspiring to her mother's customers.

Nicole was struggling and having a difficult time thinking of something original for this year's art contest. The rules stated that the project simply had to be created entirely by the student, without any adult help. There were no restrictions on size or materials. As she sat and decorated a chocolate cupcake with small animal shapes for a child's birthday party, Nicole had an incredible idea. "That's it!" she said out loud.

The next day after school, she asked her mother to teach her how to make the cupcakes and frosting. If the rules stated that the entire project had to be made without help, she would have to do it all herself. Nicole spent hours meticulously measuring the ingredients and her first batch of cupcakes turned out perfect.

In order to create the edible canvas she was imagining, Nicole would have to do some math. She doubled the batter and made one giant cupcake in a large round pan. Adjusting the baking time was tricky, but Nicole figured it out. She frosted her giant confection and then went to work to transfer her artwork from a simple sketch to the frosting.

On the night of the art show, Nicole's edible painting brought surprised looks from her friends, teachers, and the contest judges. Her oversized cupcake won first place. But the judges had to create a new category: Edible Art. After she received her ribbon, Nicole's mother cut and served her art project. Everyone agreed that it tasted as good as it looked.

Answer the questions about the reading.

1. Why did Nicole walk to the bakery shop after school every day? _____

_____

2. Nicole wasn't a very talented artist. *True* or *false*? _____

3. *Pipe* is a multiple-meaning word. In which sentence is *pipe* used the same way as in this story?
_____

   a. The plumber carried a metal pipe and his tools into the house.

   b. My father used to pipe water from our fish tank into a bucket.

   c. "Pipe down," my older sister told us. "I'm trying to study."

   d. The pastry chef loved to pipe the buttercream frosting along the edges of the cake.

4. Place a check next to the words or phrases that describe Nicole's mother.

   a. _____ patient

   b. _____ an entrepreneur, or someone who starts their own business

   c. _____ creative

   d. _____ afraid to take chances

5. Which of the above words or phrases describe Nicole? _____

6. The setting or where most of the story takes place is at _____.

   a. Nicole's school   **b.** Nicole's mother's bakery

   c. a shop near Nicole's house   **d.** Nicole and her mother's home

7. The author wrote this story to entertain his or her readers. *True* or *false*? _____

8. What do you think will happen to Nicole next? Write your own ending to the story.

_____

_____

_____

_____

_____

Who?

Characters are what make stories come alive. If an author creates good characters, his or her readers will continue to read to the end of the story to find out how life turns out for them. These characters must be believable and real. Readers don't necessarily have to like certain characters in a story, but they must be able to understand why they do the things they do.

Many authors think a long time about their characters before they even start writing about them. A writer should know more about his or her character than is actually needed to write the story.

Think about a story you can write. Now think about who your main character will be. Try to imagine that person is real and reacting to the things in his or her life. Then complete the list below, which will familiarize you with your leading character.

Name _____ Age _____

Physical appearance

_____

_____

Type of home _____ Family members _____

Pets _____ Favorite activities or hobbies _____

Favorite foods

_____

_____

Favorite color _____ Names of friends _____

Fears _____ Memories _____

Health _____ Favorite school subject _____

Other details

_____

_____

Nice to Meet You

Knowing the details of your character will help you write about him or her. Because they are what make stories so interesting, characters must be able to say words that are genuine. Their voice needs to sound like them.

First write a short paragraph that describes your character. Use the details you collected on page 134.

_____

_____

_____

_____

_____

_____

Now imagine that you are in an elevator with your character. Write a likely dialogue, or conversation, the two of you might have. Limit the conversation to four or five lines.

_____

_____

_____

_____

_____

What's New?

During every minute of every day, something is happening somewhere in the world. According to a recent study, 81 percent of all Americans find a way each day to find out what is happening worldwide. Where are they looking?

We keep up with the news in many different ways. We read newspapers and magazines. We watch morning and nightly news programs on television and listen to them on the radio. We surf the Internet for news. The study, which was conducted by the Pew Research Center for the People and the Press, was released July 2006. It outlined how Americans were getting their daily dose of information.

On a typical day, almost 60 percent of all Americans watch television news shows. That means that, out of 100 people, almost 60 of them are tuning into TV to find out what is happening in the world. The popularity of news television has dropped over the years, but local news programming still remains at the top of favorite news shows. In fact, the survey noted that hometown television news is the most commonly watched news throughout the country.

Newspapers came in second. Fifty percent of Americans read the newspaper every day. Included in that number are the people who use online newspaper sites. The study found that *The New York Times* and *USA Today* have the most popular newspaper Web sites. The most traditional form of spreading word of current events, newspapers are where the raw news becomes stories. Internet news sources often get their stories from these newspapers.

Many people still get their news from radio broadcasts. Whether they are driving in a car or working at home, about 44 out of every 100 Americans tune into radio call-in shows, news programs, and public radio stations.

Almost one-fourth of all Americans get news online. That is about 25 percent, or 25 people out of 100. Popular news sources include national television network sites, newspaper Web sites, and online news magazines. This form of communication is growing and may soon become the most widespread way in which Americans get their news.

The face of how Americans get their news is changing. How will you find out what is happening in the world today?

Answer the questions about the reading.

1. What percentage of Americans are interested in knowing what is happening in the world every day? _____

2. That's about _____ people out of every 100.

3. Place a check next to the ways in which people get their news.

a. ___ newspapers   **b.** ___ television news programs

c. ___ Internet   **d.** ___ movies

4. Out of the above news sources, which one is the most popular? _____

5. More than half of all Americans get their news from listening to the radio. *True* or *false*?

_____

6. Create a bar graph to show the percentage of Americans getting their news from each source. Make each bar a different color.

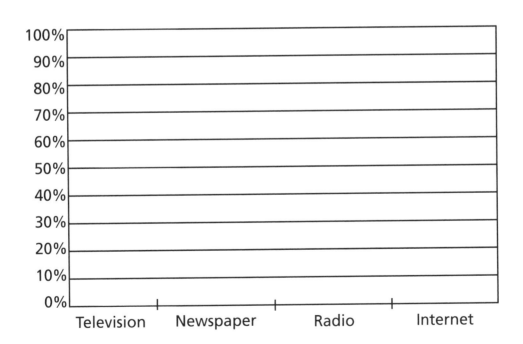

7. Look at the graph. What conclusion can you draw about how people get their news?

_____

8. How do you get your news?

_____

For the Love of Lobsters

When people think of Maine, they often think of lobsters. With about 3,500 miles of coastline, Maine lobster fishing is big business. To take advantage of one of the state's natural resources, as well as tap into the growing tourist industry, small towns along the coast host fairs, events, and contests, all using the lobster as their mascot. But one festival stands well above the rest.

It all started in 1947. That's the year when a group of people began discussing how to attract more summer tourists to Camden, a small town on the coast. The committee agreed that a marine festival would be a good idea. The group decided that they would sponsor a lobster festival that summer, which would also introduce tourists to the state's dish.

The first lobster festival offered all the lobster that anyone could eat, for just one dollar. As a result, the town lost money. They decided not to hold the fair again. But a group of young people from the Junior Chamber of Commerce of Rockland, a neighboring town, liked the idea and thought that they could make it work in their town. In 1948, they organized a parade, a concert, and a coronation ball, or beauty contest and dance. Local fishermen cooked and sold lobster, and the very first "Miss Maine Seafoods" was crowned. The two-day event was held on the first weekend in August. This is the same weekend the festival is held today.

Through the years, the fair has grown. Now the festival parade draws thousands of people and is one of the longest parades in Maine. During the 1970s and 1980s, carnival rides, games, and side shows were added to the event. But during the 1990s, festival coordinators announced that the festival would not be held anymore. However, community leaders rallied, or came together to show their support, and reorganized the event. As a result, the Maine Lobster Festival is now listed as one of the top 250 events in the United States.

The lobster festival is more than just fun and games. Much of the money that is raised during the event is donated to projects and activities that benefit the community. For example, one year the festival raised $10,000 for the Bob Gagnon Cancer Center, $12,000 for fencing at a local park, and $5,000 for the Rockland Police Department. Festival organizers have also donated funds to local schools and senior citizen centers. The entire festival is planned and run by volunteers. In fact, the planning committee begins working on the following summer's lobster festival just days after the gates close on the current year's event. If you need something fun to do this summer, check out the Maine Lobster Festival.

Answer the questions about the reading.

1. Maine has about _____ miles of coastline.

2. In Maine, lobsters are ___.
  a. not part of the state's culture
  b. a natural resource and big business
  c. kept as pets
  d. left alone to live and grow in the oceans

3. The first lobster festival was held to bring tourists into the state and to promote lobsters. *True* or *false*? _____

4. The first lobster festival was not a success. That is the effect. The cause was that ___.
  a. the town lost money by selling lobsters too cheap
  b. no one came to the event
  c. the townspeople complained and canceled it
  d. the state government told them that they couldn't hold another festival

5. After the first year's festival failed, a group of young people made it work. That group was the _____ and they organized a _____, _____, and _____.

6. Can you infer that the people of Maine like the festival and want it to continue? _____ Circle the sentence in the reading that is a clue.

7. The word *rallied* in paragraph 4 means ___.
  a. recovered from an illness
  b. scored one or more homeruns in an inning of baseball
  c. came together to show support
  d. gathered for an event

8. Money from the lobster festival helps many organizations. Place a check next to the ones mentioned in the reading.
  a. ____ Rockland Police Department
  b. ____ cancer center
  c. ____ local parks, schools, and senior citizen centers
  d. ____ a big party in November

9. Everyone who works at the lobster festival is paid. *True* or *false*? _____

Haiku to You, Too

Haiku is a form of Japanese poetry that has been around for a long time. A haiku is made up of three lines that don't rhyme. The first and last lines, however, have five syllables each. The second line has seven syllables.

Writing haiku can be more difficult than it sounds. But these simple phrases sound thoughtful and profound when read aloud. However, if you choose a subject that you know and love, writing haikus can be easy. Here's an example:

> Baseball is my game,
>
> Standing on home plate, bat up,
>
> Nothing can stop me.

Count the syllables. Five, seven, five, right? Now it's your turn. Think of your favorite people, things, and hobbies. Write a haiku. Illustrate it with a simple drawing.

_____

_____

_____

A Study of Cinquains

A cinquain is a form of poetry. It is a simple, five-line poem that follows a certain pattern:

Line 1: noun

Line 2: two adjectives

Line 3: three verbs

Line 4: descriptive phrase

Line 5: synonym for the noun in the first line

To write a cinquain, just follow those directions! Here is an example:

Books

Entertaining, enlightening

Read, devour, learn

Takes me to another place

Words

Now try writing two of your own. Remember to choose topics that you like.

All Thumbs

The next time you are riding a bus or train, or walking in a city, look around. Many people are holding onto small devices called BlackBerries. These handheld gadgets are phones, but they are also a way to communicate with other people through e-mail. As a result of spending hours typing words on a tiny keypad, many adults are suffering from "BlackBerry thumb."

We need our thumbs to grasp and hold onto things. So when doing both becomes painful, everyday tasks are difficult to complete. Imagine being unable to write with a pen, hold a baseball bat, or play video games. That is what's happening to people who spend too much time on their BlackBerries.

In the 1980s, when video games became popular, many children and teenagers began suffering from a condition called "Nintendoitis." Named because of the pain they experienced in their thumbs after playing hours of Nintendo games, young people found that they were unable to grip things. Pressing repeatedly on the buttons on a video game controller caused the tendons in the thumbs to become irritated. Thumbs were not meant to be moved that way over and over again. Even women who lived 100 years ago suffered a form of this ailment. Known officially as tendonitis, or swelling and inflammation of the tendons, women with the job of washing clothes suffered with aching thumbs. Without the luxury of a washing machine, these women would wash and ring out clothes by hand. They did this over and over again, day after day. They called it washer woman's thumb.

BlackBerry thumb is similar to Nintendoitis. They both cause intense pain and can eventually lead to loss of movement and strength in the thumb. While kids pounded on buttons with their thumbs, adults are now using theirs to text and type friends and coworkers. The more they type, the worse the condition becomes.

Experts are giving adults the same advice that they gave kids who overused their video game controllers. When your thumb begins to ache, take a break. Put ice on the area that hurts. Try not to use the device more than you have to. But there are a few things that people in severe pain can do.

Experts recommend that you first visit your doctor. Tendonitis of the thumbs is treated in many ways. Some people believe that massage helps. Others think that special balms and lotions work. But, once agan, the best way to deal with this tendonitis is to prevent it from happening in the first place. Use the BlackBerry less often. Instead of texting, talk on the phone. And turn your BlackBerry off from time to time!

Answer the questions about the reading.

1. The author compares BlackBerry thumb with a condition that occurred in the 1980s. That condition is called _____.

2. Tendonitis is _____.
    a. swelling and inflammation of the tendons   **b.** aches and pains in the legs
    c. a sore throat and headache   **d.** another word for the flu

3. This condition dates back to more than 1,000 years ago and affected women who washed clothes by hand. *True* or *false*? _____

4. BlackBerry thumb does **not** cause which of the following symptoms? _____
    a. intense pain in the thumb   **b.** swollen wrists
    c. loss of strength in the thumb   **d.** loss of movement in the thumb

5. Circle the sentence in the reading that tells what causes Nintendoitis and BlackBerry thumb.

6. What is the first thing you should do if your thumb begins to ache? _____
_____

7. Place a check next to the ways in which experts recommend treating tendonitis of the thumbs.
    a. _____ massage   **b.** _____ special balms and lotions
    c. _____ prevention   **d.** _____ all of the above

8. There are ways to avoid developing BlackBerry thumb. *True* or *false*? _____

9. Write a brief radio advertisement that tells the public how to prevent BlackBerry thumb.

_____

_____

_____

_____

10. Using some of the text from your radio advertisement, create a small ad for a local newspaper on a separate sheet of paper. Try to think of a short headline. Illustrate the ad.

Take a Deep Breath

In 2005, almost 17,000 people died in alcohol-related car accidents in the United States. People who drink alcohol should not drive a car. It is important that drunk drivers stay off the roads. Police officers have a tool that can tell almost instantly how much a person has been drinking. This helps them decide whether or not to take the person's car keys away.

When a person drinks alcohol, it is detectable in his or her breath. After the alcohol is absorbed by the mouth, throat, stomach, and intestines, it enters the bloodstream. As the blood flows through the lungs, some of the alcohol moves across the air sacs in the lung into the air. As the air is exhaled, the alcohol that is present in the bloodstream is also in the air the person just blew out.

A Breathalyzer is a portable breath-testing machine that determines what a person's blood alcohol concentration level is. It is used by police officers to determine if a driver is intoxicated, or drunk. Then he or she will know almost immediately whether or not there is a reason to arrest the driver.

Using a chemical reaction that causes a color change when mixed with alcohol, a Breathalyzer has a mouthpiece, a tube through which the person breathes, and a sample chamber where the air goes. To measure the amount of alcohol in a person's breath, he or she simply breathes into the device. The air sample bubbles through a vial that contains chemicals such as sulfuric acid, potassium dichromate, silver nitrate, and water. As the air passes through the reddish-orange mixture, it changes to a green color if alcohol is present. The shade of green depends on how much a person has been drinking.

By looking at the meter on the Breathalyzer, the police officer conducting the test knows the exact concentration of alcohol in the driver's blood. In the United States, the legal standard for intoxication is 0.08%. According to the American Medical Association, a person can become impaired by alcohol if his or her level hits 0.05. But if the results of the Breathalyzer show that someone's blood alcohol concentration level is 0.10, for example, the police officer can arrest him or her for drunk driving.

Using this quick and easy device, police officers are making our roads safer. By arresting people who are drinking and driving, they are also saving lives.

Answer the questions about the reading.

1. People who are drinking alcohol should not drive a car. *True* or *false*? _____

2. Almost _____ people died in 2005 as the result of alcohol-related car accidents.

3. A synonym for the word *absorbed* in paragraph 2 is ____.
   a. having flowed out of something   **b.** having been soaked up
   c. having been breathed in   **d.** having been used to find blood alcohol levels

4. Place a check next to the statements that are true about Breathalyzers.
   a. ____ They are used by police officers to determine if someone has been drinking alcohol.
   b. ____ They are small machines used by dentists.
   c. ____ They are portable breath-testing machines.
   d. ____ They calculate a person's blood alcohol level.

5. Number the steps in the Breathalyzer process in the correct order.
   ____ The air sample mixes with chemicals.
   ____ A police officer suspects that a driver has been drinking alcohol.
   ____ The police officer asks the person to breathe into a mouthpiece.
   ____ If the mixture turns green, the police officer reads the meter to determine the blood alcohol level.

6. People who have been drinking alcohol have a higher blood alcohol concentration level. *True* or *false*? _____

7. Police officers use the Breathalyzer to make our roads _____.

8. When someone is *intoxicated*, he or she ____.
   a. is having pains in the chest   **b.** has had too much alcohol to drink
   c. is in the middle of a panic attack   **d.** needs insulin

9. Is an air sample a large or small amount of air? _____

10. Do you think it unfair for a police officer to ask someone to take a Breathalyzer test? Explain your opinion.

_____

_____

The Telescope

"I want you to write a story." Those seven words can sometimes cause someone to break into a sweat. There is so much to write about. There is so much out there. Often the biggest roadblock to a story is figuring out what to write about.

If you ever feel overwhelmed by such a writing project, try this. Find a cardboard roll from a used roll of paper towels. Hold it up to your eye like a pirate peering through his telescope. Then look. Turn your head left and right. Search for something that will fit inside that small circle. You will know it when you see it.

Look. Focus. Write what you are thinking. For example:

"I see a bookshelf. I wonder what is on it. I've looked at the books on that shelf all year, but this is the first time I ever really noticed it. There are only three blue books in a row. The next one is red. The one beside that one is tan. I wonder who has read them, how many people have opened those books and read the stories that are there to be told. I imagine my dad as a kid, in his bedroom, in his hometown, reading those stories and feeling inspired. I think I want to write about my dad when he was younger."

Now it's your turn. First use your telescope. Focus on something near you. Then write your thoughts in the circle below. They could be the start to a great story!

The Camera

Now you have the idea for a story inside the circle on page 146. It might be about what you saw outside the window beside your seat. It might be about the poster on the wall. Whatever it is, you wrote the idea for a story. Let's see if you can "pitch" it to a movie producer.

Pitch is a multiple-meaning word. Sometimes it means to throw a baseball. This time it means to tell your story to someone. Write a paragraph explaining your story and why it would make a great movie. If you don't think it would make a great movie, would it make one super scene in a movie? You can write about that instead.

Brrrrr!

Temperature alone is not enough information to properly dress yourself for a day outside during the winter. Meteorologists tell us that how hard the wind is blowing plays a big role in how cold the air really feels when you may be standing on the top of a ski slope. Wind chill is what they call this combination of frostiness and breeziness.

When you watch the local weather on television, the weatherperson usually tells you how warm or cold it is outside. That is the temperature of the air in the town where you live. Temperature is the measure of how much heat is present in something. But if the wind is blowing, that temperature is not as accurate as you think.

Anytime we go outdoors into the cold, we lose heat. That happens to all warm objects when they are exposed to cold air. If the wind is blowing hard, the object will lose heat at a faster rate. In fact, the greater the wind speed, the more quickly that object will lose its heat. While a warm mug of hot chocolate won't feel the cold, humans certainly do.

Human beings' bodies sense when they lose heat. This temperature we feel is called sensible temperature. Only on a windy day, the temperature outside may feel a lot colder than the temperature reported by the weatherperson. This phenomenon usually occurs when the wind is blowing. Brrr. Wind chill.

Wind chill is defined as the rate of heat loss from skin that is exposed to both cold and wind. As the wind speeds up, heat leaves the body faster. This lowers the temperature of the part of the body that is open to the elements. When meteorologists calculate wind chill, we get a better estimate of how cold the air outside really feels. Wind chill is not a temperature, but a measure of the rate of heat loss. It is based on how cold the air temperature is and how fast the wind is blowing.

Using a wind chill calculator, weather experts can determine the wind chill index. For example, if the outside temperature is 32 degrees Fahrenheit and the wind is blowing at 30 miles per hour, the wind chill index is 18. That means that the air outside will feel like 18 degrees.

Knowing the wind chill is important, especially for people who spend a lot of time outside in the cold weather months. A lower wind chill means that frostbite and hypothermia, which occurs when the inside of your body can't maintain its normal temperature, can develop more quickly. Checking the wind chill can help you dress so that, when you do go out, you can feel warm and enjoy your time safely.

Answer the questions about the reading.

1. Wind chill is ____.
   a. the temperature of the air
   b. the measure of how fast the wind is blowing
   c. the rate of heat loss from skin that is exposed to cold and wind
   d. how cold you are when you step outdoors

2. A *meteorologist* is another word for a _____.

3. Temperature is the measure of how much heat is in something. *True* or *false*? _____

4. When we are warm and go out into the cold air, we ____.
   a. lose heat   **b.** stay just as warm
   c. keep all our heat inside as long as we wear hats   **d.** get very cold, very fast

5. When people lose heat, they sense it and feel colder. What is this kind of temperature called?
   _____

6. When the wind is blowing harder, the body loses heat more slowly. *True* or *false*?

   _____

7. Meteorologists use a wind chill calculator to ____.
   a. figure out the air temperature   **b.** determine how long it will remain cold
   c. determine if it will snow   **d.** figure out the wind chill index

8. Is it important to know what the wind chill index is? _____ Circle the sentence that is
   a clue.

9. Name two weather-related conditions that could be harmful:
   _____ and _____

10. Do you think meteorologists like their jobs? Why or why not?

   _____

   _____

   _____

   _____

From Playing Music to Diplomacy

She worked hard to learn how to play the piano as a young girl. With that same determination, Condoleezza Rice woke up every day in Washington, D.C., and tackled her duties as the first African American woman to serve as U.S. Secretary of State.

Born on November 14, 1954, in Birmingham, Alabama, Condoleezza was the only child of John and Angelena Rice. Her father was a minister and her mother was a science and music teacher.

Growing up during the 1960s was difficult, and she remembers being treated unkindly or unfairly because of the color of her skin. She was once barred from entering an amusement park because of her race. She also lost a good friend when she was eight years old: young Denise McNair was killed when a group of people bombed the church she was attending at the time. That event made a lifetime impression on Condoleezza and she spoke about it in her speech at Vanderbilt University in 2004.

In 1967, she and her family moved to Denver, Colorado, where she attended a private, all-girls Catholic high school. She studied the piano and later graduated from the University of Denver, the University of Notre Dame, and the Graduate School of International Studies at the University of Denver.

Condoleezza was a founding member of the Center for a New Generation, which is an educational support fund for schools in California. She was also the Vice President of the Boys and Girls Club. She has served on many boards of big corporations and under President George H. W. Bush from 1989 to 1991 on the National Security Council.

Condoleezza Rice became the sixty-sixth secretary of state and the first black woman to serve in that position in January 2005. Each day she was the principal adviser to President George W. Bush on foreign policy. She negotiated with other countries, granted passports to Americans, attended conferences, and provided information to Americans about what is happening in foreign countries. Condoleezza also kept custody of the Great Seal of the United States and prepared and published treaties and international documents.

In her free time, Condoleezza managed to continue to play the piano. Up until her second year in college, Condoleezza planned to be a concert pianist. She practiced hard and attended special music programs and schools. Sometimes she missed playing the piano as much as she would like to, but because she grew up with the belief that music is something that anyone can love all throughout life, she is happy to play when she can.

Answer the questions about the reading.

1. Condoleezza Rice is the first black woman to serve as U.S. _____.

2. Place a check next to the sentences that are true of Condoleezza's life.
    a. _____ She was an only child.
    b. _____ She was born on November 14, 1954.
    c. _____ She remembers a happy childhood when she could go and do whatever she wanted to.
    d. _____ Her good friend was killed when the church she attended was bombed.

3. Describe an incident in Condoleezza's childhood that was related to the color of her skin.
_____
_____

4. Condoleezza remembers other times when she was treated unkindly. *True* or *false*?
_____
_____

5. Condoleezza grew up in the 1960s. She remembers things that happened to her because she was black. Make an inference about how black people were treated during that decade.
_____
_____

6. Which of these sentences does **not** describe one of Condoleezza Rice's responsibilities as Secretary of State? _____
    a. She attended conferences.
    b. She updated Americans on what is happening in other places.
    c. She signed laws so they can be carried out.
    d. She granted passports to Americans.

7. Does Condoleezza still like to play the piano? _____ Underline the sentences in the story that are clues.

8. On a separate sheet of paper, write a brief paragraph that describes Condoleezza Rice. Include information about her childhood and some of her accomplishments as an adult.

What's the Point?

The point of view of a story is the position from where a story is told. There are two common types of point of view. A story written in the first person means that the writer is telling the story. The narrator uses the words *I* or *we*, although he or she doesn't always have to be a main character. Here is an example of first-person point of view:

I spent all day yesterday thinking about the science fair. I knew that the project I would submit had to be original. I knew it had to be really great. But I just couldn't think of an experiment that interested me. I went to the school library and decided to take one last look around. Maybe I will find something inspiring there.

The third-person point of view means that an outside narrator tells the events of the story, using words like *he* or *she*. The following paragraph is the same story as above, but written in third person.

Kelly spent all yesterday day thinking about the science fair. She wanted it to be both original and great. She was just having such a difficult time finding an experiment that interested her. After days of struggling and being unable think of a project idea, she walked to the school's library. As she wandered through the bookshelves, she hoped to find something fascinating.

Write *F* or *T* next to each sentence to tell whether it is written in first or third person.

1. _____ I rode my bicycle to town hall to get a copy of the law.

2. _____ I was really enjoying the new book I was reading.

3. _____ Joseph walked over to the curb and picked up the shiny penny.

4. _____ The best part about going to my Aunt Barbara's house for dinner is sitting at the table with the adults.

5. _____ Thomas and Matthew played basketball for opposing teams.

Point Out Another View

Writing the same story from different points of view can be challenging. But this exercise also provides an interesting way to understand the story from someone else's perspective.

Read the following paragraph, which is written in the third person.

Jake and Stephen couldn't wait for their first snowboarding lesson. The twelve-year-old twins were so excited that they were ready to leave their house an hour before their lesson! By the time they arrived at Mount Peter Ski Area, Jake was ecstatic. He grabbed his new snowboard and raced toward the instructor, who was talking to three other students. Stephen stepped out of the car more slowly and carefully picked up his snowboard. He took a deep breath and looked up the ski slope. The hill looked a lot steeper than he had imagined it would.

Choose one character from the story and rewrite the paragraph from his point of view, in the first person. It is okay to make inferences from what you've read to make the story more interesting.

_____

_____

_____

_____

_____

_____

_____

_____

_____

_____

How Do They Do It?

They weigh thousands of pounds and carry hundreds of people at a time. They start out on the ground at one place and end up on the ground at another. In between, they soar above the clouds, thousands of miles above earth. How do planes fly and stay in the air?

Airplanes can fly because of a basic law discovered by a Dutch scientist named Daniel Bernoulli. According to Bernoulli's Principle, airplanes stay in the air because the force that is keeping them up is greater than the force that is pushing them down. It's all about lift and drag.

Lift is the upward movement of air pressure as a plane moves through the sky. The faster an airplane goes, the greater the lift. To understand this, picture a bird. An airplane's wings are similar. They are curved on top and flat on the bottom. Because the shortest distance between two places is a straight line, the length from the front to the back of the bottom part of the wing is shorter than the top, curved part. Air molecules move along the wing as the plane moves forward. They start at the front and meet at the back. But because the molecules must move faster along the top of the wing in order to meet up with the molecules that are moving along the bottom, which is shorter than the top, pressure is created. The pressure on the bottom of the wing is greater than on the top. Bernoulli found that this difference in pressure causes lift, or the ability of the wing to move up. As an airplane speeds up, the air flowing over the wings increases. That makes the lift greater.

Drag is the force that resists the forward motion of the airplane. It affects how pilots maneuver their planes and how fuel-efficient the planes are. If you hold up a piece of cardboard vertically on a windy day, you can feel the force of drag. If you turn the cardboard horizontally, you can feel a decrease in drag. By conducting this simple experiment, you can see how the cardboard is pushed backward when it is held flat against the wind. But if it is rotated toward the ground, the wind pushes it up and back. This is what happens to airplanes. With engines to propel the jet forward, the plane takes flight!

The aerodynamic principles that explain the effect of motion on air are critical to engineers who design airplanes. They must understand movement, lift, and drag. So the next time you look up into the sky, think about all those tiny air molecules holding up that great big plane.

Answer the questions about the reading.

1. The Dutch scientist who discovered the basic law of flight was named

_____.

2. Airplanes can take off air because of lift. *True* or *false*? _____

3. Lift is ____.

  a. the pressure at the bottom of an airplane's wing

  b. the upward movement of air pressure as a plane flies through the sky

  c. when air molecules move along the plane's wings

  d. picking things quickly and holding them up high

4. In the explanation of lift, what is an airplane compared to?_____

5. Bernoulli's Principle states that ____.

  a. the force that keeps the airplane in the air is greater than the force that is keeping it down

  b. airplanes fly because they weigh less than air

  c. the wings of an airplane are shaped like a bird's wings

  d. the shortest distant between two lines is a straight line

6. Place a check next to the statements that are true.

  a. _____ The distance on the top part of an airplane's wing is longer than the bottom.

  b. _____ Air molecules have to move more quickly to move across the top of a plane's wing and meet those below.

  c. _____ As an airplane goes faster, the air flowing over the wing decreases.

  d. _____ The difference in air pressure between the top and bottom of the wings creates lift.

7. How does the author help the reader understand drag? _____
_____

8. Engineers who design airplanes must understand _____,
_____, and _____.

9. Aerodynamic principles are ____.

  a. rules that explain how earth turns

  b. laws only that tell about how birds fly

  c. rules that explain the effect of motion on air

  d. theories that describe how water and air affect motion

The Generals' Horses

America in the 1800s was a much different place from how it is now. People relied on horses for transportation, recreation, and work. During the Civil War years, people became more dependent on the strength, courage, and endurance of these animals.

Horses could help in many ways, and they became as important as soldiers during the war. They carried messengers, commanding officers, and equipment. They carried artillery, or weapons. Horses were muscular and able to run quickly across a battlefield. Their loyalty to their masters made them dedicated companions. Soldiers worked hard to take care of the horses they rode. They made sure to feed them well and set up camp next to clean water sources. Many soldiers spent their evenings feeding, watering, and taking care of their horses before getting themselves ready for bed.

Because going to war was a tough job for the horses, they were trained and tested first. Horses between the ages of five and seven years old were sent to the battlefield. If they were calm during tense situations and followed directions from their riders, they were also chosen to go to war. Horses that were also very sturdy and strong were chosen to carry generals.

Many Civil War horses pulled wagons, ambulances, and cannons. Those chosen to transport generals served an important job. Generals were highly respected and thus treated in more superior ways than soldiers. Many of them rode horses to be higher than their troops. From his higher seat a general could not only monitor his troops, but also spot potential dangers more quickly than if he were marching on the ground. Many Civil War horses that belonged to generals became famous.

General Thomas J. Jackson rode an eleven-year-old horse named Old Sorrel. He bought the small horse for his wife as a gift in 1861, but he took him to war instead. For more than two years, the general and his horse were together. Old Sorrel was even beside Jackson as he died at the battle of Chancellorsville in 1863. After that, the horse was sent to live at the school where General Jackson taught, the Virginia Military Institute.

Perhaps the most famous Civil War horse was Traveler. He was five years old when General Robert E. Lee purchased him in 1862. He was sixteen hands high. That's about five feet and three inches tall. General Lee rode Traveler through most of the war, including at the Battle of Gettysburg. When the war ended, Traveler and General Lee went to live at Washington College. When the general died, his horse marched in his funeral procession.

There are many more famous Civil War horses, of course, and each one was as brave as the next.

Answer the questions about the reading.

1. Place a check next to what people relied on horses for during the 1800s.

   a. _____ work   **b.** _____ food

   c. _____ recreation   **d.** _____ transportation

2. Horses became as important as soldiers during the Civil War. *True* or *false*? _____

3. Name three jobs of horses during the Civil War:

_____

_____

4. Circle the words or phrases in the word bank that describe the Civil War horses.

   muscular   strong   slow   easily frightened   dedicated   sturdy

5. Place a check next to the ways that soldiers ensured their horses were healthy.

   a. _____ They let them run free sometimes.

   b. _____ They watered and cared for them every night.

   c. _____ They set up camp near clean water sources.

   d. _____ They fed them well.

6. Horses were hardly ever tested before they were sent to the battlefield. *True* or *false*?

_____

7. One of the biggest advantages that Civil War generals had by riding horses was that

_____

8. Many Civil War generals' horses became famous. Perhaps the most famous one was

_____

9. A horse that is sixteen hands high is _____.

   a. five feet tall   **b.** six feet and three inches tall

   c. five feet and three inches tall   **d.** four feet and nine inches tall

10. Using what you read and what you know about horses, why do you think that soldiers and generals became so attached to their horses?

_____

_____

Imagine the Image

Imagery in writing involves the senses. An author creates this imagery, or dramatic description, by using sensory words. To help the reader create mental pictures, the author can also use figurative language, such as similes and metaphors.

A **simile** is a comparison of two things that uses the word *like* or *as*.

Example: Be careful when walking today, because the sandy sidewalk is as slippery as ice.

Underline the word or phrase that is being described by the simile in each sentence. Draw brackets around the word or phrase that it is being compared to.

Example: Be careful walking today, the sandy <u>sidewalk</u> is as [slippery as ice].

1. Kim's smile is as sweet as candy.

2. My dog is big, but he is as gentle as a lamb.

3. My teacher told us that taking drugs is like playing with fire.

4. The boy's temper was as explosive as fireworks.

5. The bad news hit me like a ton of bricks.

A **metaphor** also describes something by comparing it to something else. But metaphors state that something *is* something else.

Example: The baby was an angel in his arms.

Write *S* or *M* next to each sentence to tell whether it is a simile or a metaphor.

6. _____The girl's mean words were fuel to the fire.

7. _____ My life is a dream.

8. _____ As quiet as a mouse, the cat walked through the room.

9. _____ The boy's questions produced a river of doubt.

10. _____ Jan's teeth are as white as snow.

Up Close and Personification

Another form of imagery is personification. Authors use personification to give human traits and qualities to inanimate objects.

Example: My computer loves to crash.

Underline the word or words that show personification in each sentence.

1. My alarm clock told me that it was time to get up.

2. The sunlight danced on the windowsill.

3. My mother's car coughed and sputtered when she started it.

4. The light rain kissed my face as I walked home.

5. I heard the wind whispering in the trees.

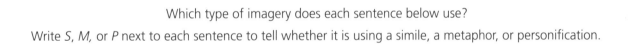

Which type of imagery does each sentence below use?
Write *S, M,* or *P* next to each sentence to tell whether it is using a simile, a metaphor, or personification.

6. _____ The new boy in class is as sly as a fox.

7. _____ The blanket wrapped its warmth around me.

8. _____ The warm sand called to me.

9. _____ He said his love was like a red rose.

10. _____ I was so sick that my legs were rubber.

11. _____ The old man was as tough as nails.

12. _____ My grandmother said that clothes need to breathe.

13. _____ The camera hates me.

14. _____ My mother was as proud as a peacock.

15. _____ "Water is my friend," said Toni.

This Is a Brain on Drugs

The brain has a very big job. During every second, the brain reads signals from your body and sends out information that keeps you thinking, walking, talking, and breathing. If the brain were in a movie, it would be the star. Naturally, taking care of the brain should be one of your most important jobs.

Your brain weighs about three pounds. It has different systems that process all kinds of information. Parts of the brain called lobes process information from your sense organs. The brain stem, which is located at the base of your brain, controls the things you never think about, such as breathing and the way your heart beats. The cerebellum takes care of all the things you learn once and then never think about again. These are things like throwing a baseball or staying balanced while you walk.

Your brain's most significant duty is processing information. There are billions of brain cells called neurons in your brain. Each one of these neurons has up to a thousand tiny branches, or axons, that reach out and communicate with other neurons. As a message, which is like a tiny electrical impulse, jumps from one axon to another, a chemical is released. This chemical is called a neurotransmitter. Your brain releases many different neurotransmitters every day.

The amazing thing about your brain is that more axons are created as you learn more new things. With more of these threadlike branches in your brain, the neurons can communicate with each other even more efficiently. In short, the more you use your brain, the better it gets. But what happens to the brain when someone decides to use drugs?

The first time someone uses a drug like marijuana, cocaine, or nicotine, which is found in cigarettes, a flood of dopamine is produced. Dopamine is a chemical neurotransmitter released in one part of the brain. That chemical causes feelings of pleasure, like when you hit a home run or eat an ice cream cone on a hot day. Because your brain is so smart, it immediately reacts to the overabundance of dopamine. Neurons start reducing the number of dopamine receptors and as a result the brain produces less of it. Sometimes drugs like marijuana, cocaine, and nicotine cause neurons to die.

Without a full supply of dopamine, you can feel depressed or unhappy. This is how drug abuse begins. The person needs the drug to feel happy again. Because the drug produces more dopamine, he or she starts to feel less sad. As time goes on and the person takes more and more drugs, the brain becomes tolerant. More amounts of the drug are now needed to create the same effect. This is called drug addiction. Drug addiction is a deadly disease. The best thing to do for your brain is to stay far away from drugs.

Answer the questions about the reading.

1. Taking good care of your brain is one of your most important jobs. *True* or *false*?

_____

2. Your brain's most significant duty is _____.

3. Match each term in the first column to its definition in the second column.

neurons   a chemical released by the brain

axons   brain cells

neurotransmitter   a neurotransmitter causing feelings of pleasure

dopamine   tiny branches connected to neurons

4. As you learn more things, your brain uses up axons. This makes you less intelligent over time. *True* or *false*? _____

5. When someone takes drugs for the first time, the brain produces a lot of _____.

6. When the brain recognizes an overabundance of dopamine, it _____.
   a. doesn't produce any more, ever
   b. reduces the amount of dopamine it produces
   c. produces more dopamine
   d. produces dopamine and other neurotransmitters to balance the chemicals

7. Sometimes drugs like marijuana, cocaine, and nicotine can cause neurons to die. *True* or *false*?

_____

8. When your brain doesn't have enough dopamine, you might feel _____.
   happy   excited   depressed   afraid

9. The need for more and more drugs to feel happy again is called _____.

10. Do you agree that drug addiction is a deadly disease? Why or why not?

_____

_____

What Luck!

Kelly couldn't believe her luck. She had only dreamed of being in the movies, but today she was going to finally get her chance. She thought she would burst. She hung up the telephone and screeched.

"I am going to be a star!" she shrieked.

Lisa and Joseph turned from their chess game and smiled. "You got the part?" asked Lisa. "When do you start?"

Kelly grabbed her backpack and left quickly. But not before she told her best friends about the advertisement she answered in the local newspaper. It was so small that she almost missed it. She called the number and talked to Rob, the New York University Film School student who was making a movie in the big barn near Kelly's house. She got the part of the cleaning lady without even auditioning, which is trying out for the part.

Kelly's mom drove her to the first rehearsal, which turned out to be not a rehearsal at all. The film school gave its students two weeks to write, direct, and make a movie. Rob's was about a group of cats who lived in a barn. Because he grew up in Center Falls, he knew exactly the place where he would film his story.

"I'll be back to pick you up at around noon," her mom shouted as Kelly raced toward the signs that said, "If you're an actor, step this way."

As Kelly walked toward the barn door, she saw Lisa and Joseph. "Surprise," shouted Joseph. "We got parts, too. We're extras."

Kelly was relieved to see some friendly faces. The extras were jammed into one side of the barn and the people with speaking parts were on the other side. In the center was an elaborate set, or scenery, of a living room. Rob walked around authoritatively, shouting orders and joking with other students who were there to help him. After the makeup and costume people did their jobs, the actors were ready for the first run-through.

The problem was that there was no script. Rob simply told the actors the story and then asked them to do what they thought they should do. It turned out that middle-school kids pretending to be cats all just meow and chase yarn. Kelly's role was to clean, and so that's what she did. The whole play took about five minutes for Rob and his camera crew to film. "That's a wrap!," he then shouted.

Kelly looked at Lisa, who was tangled in about 300 feet of pink yarn, and Joseph, who was pretending to stalk a mouse, and laughed. *If this is what it is like to break into show business*, Kelly thought, *then count me in*.

"That was so much fun, but not at all what I thought it would be," Kelly told her mother when she picked her up. "It was confusing and noisy and no one knew what they were supposed to do. But it was fun." Kelly smiled.

Answer the questions about the story.

1. What is the name of Kelly's hometown? _____

2. How did Kelly feel when she learned that she landed a small part in a film? _____

    sad   excited   unsure   worried

3. Circle the words in the word bank that you think describe Kelly.

           hopeful   friendly   anxious   outgoing   unhappy   motivated   angry

4. Rob chose to film his movie in a barn in Center Falls because he had grown up in that town. *True* or *false*? _____

5. To *audition* means to _____.

    a. sing a song   **b.** try out for a part in a play

    c. read aloud in front of a group   **d.** learn to play an instrument

6. How much time were the film students given to write and make a movie? _____

    a. two weeks   **b.** two days

    c. three months   **d.** two months

7. What was Rob's play about? _____

_____

8. Was Kelly happy to see Lisa and Joseph at the barn? _____ Circle the sentence that is the clue.

9. Why might not having a script for a movie be a problem?

_____

_____

10. Visualize the five minutes of filming. Write a few sentences describing what you see.

_____

_____

_____

_____

Apples and Oranges

When you compare and contrast, you look closely at two or more things to discover what they have in common and what is different between them. When you read, comparing and contrasting characters in stories helps you to understand why they act the way they do. To *compare* means "to find the things that are the same about two or more objects." To *contrast* means "to find the things that are different between them."

Think about an apple and an orange. Consider what they are, how they are used, and what they look like and smell like. Think of everything you can about the two pieces of fruit. You might want to examine an actual apple and orange, too.

Complete the compare-and-contrast diagram below. Add as many details as you can think of.

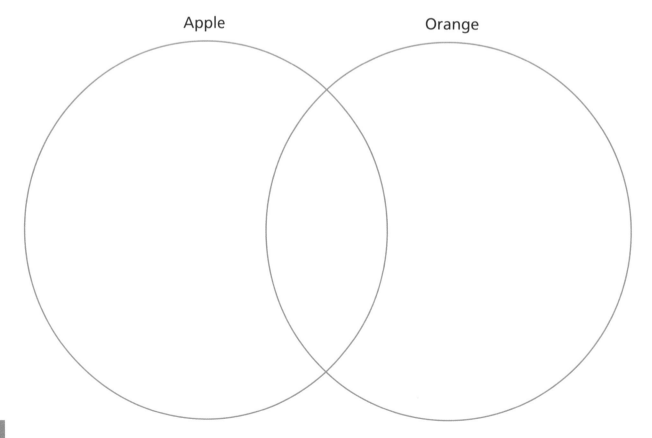

Apple   Orange

Comparatively Speaking

Comparing and contrasting two objects helps you to analyze and think about them. But comparing and contrasting two things can also help make your writing more descriptive.

For example, compare baseball and football. They are both sports. They are played in stadiums. Their seasons end with big games that determine who the best team is. They are team sports. The players wear uniforms.

Next, contrast baseball and football. The balls are different. Football players wear a lot more protective gear. The rules are different. Each sport is played with a different number of players on the teams. In baseball there are nine innings and in football there are four quarters.

Now think of two things, like day and night; painting and drawing; walking and running; snowboarding and skiing. Then compare and contrast them below.

Compare

_____

_____

_____

Contrast

_____

_____

_____

Now write a paragraph describing both.

_____

_____

_____

_____

_____

The Real CSI

Crime scene investigations are popular on television. But what really goes on behind the scenes after a crime is committed? Take a look at some real heroes.

Police officers are usually the first professionals to arrive at a crime scene. If the person who committed the crime is still there, the officers will make an arrest. If an ambulance is needed, it will be called. The police officers are the ones responsible for securing the scene so that no evidence is destroyed or tampered with. That might mean wrapping yellow tape around the entire area and keeping people away so that nothing is touched or moved. Then the police officers call the crime scene investigation unit.

Because the police have already secured the scene, the investigator can get right down to business. The first thing to do is to walk through the scene and take a thorough look at what happened. This helps the investigator generate a theory about what happened, based only on what he or she sees. The investigator does not touch anything during this initial walk-through.

Meanwhile, more professionals arrive at the scene. The district attorney usually shows up to see if the team needs a special document called a search warrant to move forward. If they do, the district attorney goes to the judge and gets one. If the crime is a murder, the medical examiner must be there to determine the cause of death. Detectives interview witnesses. If expert opinions are needed, scientists and psychologists may be asked to come to the scene.

The crime scene investigator takes photographs and draws sketches of everything that he or she sees during a second walk-through. After the scene is documented, he or she carefully begins to collect items that may become evidence, or proof. The items are tagged, written into a log, or notebook, and packaged so that they arrive at the crime laboratory without being damaged. Once at the lab, the crime lab technician uses many different tests and techniques to come to a conclusion. What goes on at the lab is called forensic science. Many crime scene investigators have training in forensic science. That means they have the ability to use medical knowledge to determine the cause of death or injury.

The investigation of a crime scene involves many professionals who must work as a team to figure out what happened. In many cases, what we see on television is just a snapshot of what really occurs.

Answer the questions about the reading.

1. Which of the following sentences is a good summary of the reading? _____
    a. Crime scene investigations are popular on television.
    b. What goes on at the lab is called forensic science.
    c. The investigation of a crime scene involves many professionals who must work as a team to figure out what happened.
    d. Police officers are responsible for securing the scene so that no evidence is destroyed or tampered with.

2. _____ are the first professionals to arrive at a crime scene.

3. *Securing the scene* means _____.
    a. letting everyone take a look
    b. walking through and keeping track of things that are seen
    c. yellow taping the area and keeping people away
    d. taking photographs

4. A synonym for the word *evidence* in paragraph 2 is _____.
    lies   pictures   notepads   proof

5. It is important to secure a crime scene so that the criminal can't come back. *True* or *false*?

_____

6. Number the steps in the correct order.
    _____ The crime scene investigator takes photographs and draws sketches.
    _____ The evidence is sent to the crime laboratory.
    _____ The crime scene investigator does an initial walk-through without touching anything.
    _____ Detectives interview people at the crime scene.

7. What does the district attorney do? _____

8. Forensic science is the use of _____.
    a. medical knowledge to determine the cause of a crime
    b. knowledge of plants and animals to learn more about the world
    c. books and magazines to understand how things work
    d. data to analyze information

Up, Up, and Away

Have you ever wondered what it might be like to ride into space in a rocket ship? Or what it would feel like to see the entire Earth through a small window, illuminated only by the light of the sun? If you have ever dreamed of taking your place in the history books beside Alan Shepard and Sally Ride, then you know what it feels like to want to be an astronaut.

When the National Aeronautics and Space Administration, or NASA, started its space exploration program in 1959, there were only seven trained astronauts in the entire United States. That number has grown immensely, thanks to young people who dream of reaching the stars.

NASA receives thousands of applications from people all over the world who want to train to become astronauts. Only about 100 men and women are chosen every two years for an intensive training program that takes long hours of studying and lots of commitment. If you want to be an astronaut, now is the time to start.

According to NASA officials, students who are considering applying to the astronaut training program should first read everything they can about astronauts and space. Then they should learn all they can about American history and watch the news to stay current with what's going on in the world. Astronauts need to be able to work well with others and be a team player. Playing sports and becoming involved in scouting are two ways to gain experience in working cooperatively with others.

Future astronauts study hard and do the very best they possibly can in high school and college. It is important to NASA that its astronauts are also well-rounded citizens. That means interested students should become involved in projects they love, hold summer jobs, and gain as much experience as they can in life. Once a student qualifies, he or she completes an application to the Johnson Space Center in Houston, Texas. More than 4,000 students apply every two years. The center asks about 120 applicants to spend a week at the center undergoing interviews, medical examinations, and orientation sessions.

The Astronaut Selection Board chooses students who have done exceptionally well in school. They choose students who have strong problem-solving skills and the ability to communicate and work well with others. Motivation, experience, and the ability to adapt, or adjust and fit, are also important characteristics. Then, the chosen students become astronauts-in-training.

The voyage into space begins with a dream. Followed up by lots of hard work, enthusiasm, and experience, young people who imagine themselves in space can start shooting for the stars now.

Answer the questions about the reading.

1. The National Aeronautics and Space Administration started its space exploration program in the year _____.

2. Place a check next to the statements that are true.
    a. _____ NASA receives thousands of applications.
    b. _____ NASA chooses about 100 men and women every two years.
    c. _____ There were hundreds of astronauts in 1959.
    d. _____ Becoming an astronaut is an easy thing to do.

3. A well-rounded citizen is someone who_____.
    a. can recite the Constitution of the United States
    b. participates in many activities to gain varied experience
    c. knows facts about America
    d. reads about history

4. If you want to become an astronaut, NASA officials recommend that you start now.
    True or *false*? _____

5. Number the steps for becoming an astronaut in the correct order.
    _____ Complete an application to the Johnson Space Center in Houston.
    _____ Play sports, volunteer, and study hard while you are in school.
    _____ Read everything you can about becoming an astronaut.
    _____ Work hard and you may be chosen as an astronaut-in-training.

6. Every two years, more than _____ students apply to the Johnson Space Center, but only _____ applicants are asked to go to the center.

7. The word *adapt* in paragraph 6 means _____ .
    a. adjust or fit   **b.** imply   **c.** hold a job   **d.** change

8. List as many characteristics as you can that describe the students chosen by the Astronaut Selection Board to become astronauts.

_____

_____

9. Circle the sentence in the reading that is the author's opinion.

Apply to Go High!

As part of the Johnson Space Center application process, each student who wants to go to Houston and become an astronaut-in-training must write an essay about himself or herself. The essay should describe why the applicant wants to be an astronaut and how he or she will achieve this dream.

Pretend that you are applying for the astronaut training program. Write your essay here. Don't forget to include a little bit about yourself and some of the extracurricular activities you are involved in. Feel free to talk about someone whom you admire. Let the selection board know that you plan to work hard and are dedicated to succeeding.

Continue your essay on another sheet of paper, if needed. Good luck!

And the Winner Is...

Now pretend you are a member of the Astronaut Selection Board for the Johnson Space Center. You just finished reading the essay on page 170. List the positive attributes, or personality characteristics, that you believe would help that student succeed in the program.

_____

_____

_____

_____

_____

_____

Now write a short acceptance letter to yourself. Give the reasons why you were chosen to travel to Houston, Texas, for the astronaut-in-training program. Congratulate yourself and describe some of the things you will do when you get there.

_____

_____

_____

_____

_____

_____

_____

_____

Locks, Lakes, and Channels

Traveling from one side of America to the other by yacht or huge ship is easy today, thanks to the Panama Canal, a series of locks, lakes, and channels built in the early 1900s. The Panama Canal is a major canal designed to carry ships through the Isthmus of Panama in Central America. An isthmus is a narrow strip of land that is bordered on both sides by water. The canal connects the Atlantic and Pacific Oceans and cuts about 8,000 miles off a ship's journey by allowing the ship to sail through Central America instead of around the southern tip of South America. Before the Panama Canal was built, ocean vessels traveling from New York City to San Francisco, California, had to sail about 14,000 miles altogether around Cape Horn. With the shortcut, the trip is now about 5,200 miles long.

Construction on the canal started in 1904. After 10 years of building, the Panama Canal officially opened on August 15, 1914. Since then, hundreds of thousands of ships have used the canal. More than 14,000 ships pass through the canal each year.

The canal consists of 17 artificial lakes, channels, and three sets of locks. It is like a two-lane highway, only made of water. In order to cross Panama, a ship enters the first set of locks. These locks act as water elevators that lift the ships to 21 meters above sea level. That is the level of Gatun Lake. The ship then sails across the lake and enters more locks. The last lock lowers the ship back to sea level on the other side of the Isthmus of Panama where it sails back out into the ocean. The ship needs about nine hours to travel through the canal.

But how does it all really work? When a ship is positioned to enter the locks, the valves in the first chamber open. Gravity forces the water to flow out so that the ship can sail into the first chamber. Once inside, valves are opened and water from the second chamber flows into the first. This brings the water level up so that the ship can continue through. The gates open and the ship enters the next chamber. Then the gates are closed behind it. Valves are opened and water from the third chamber flows into the second one, causing the water level to rise again. This lifts the ship so that it can enter the next chamber. The valves are opened again and water gushes into the third chamber. This lifts the ship so that it can then enter the Gatun Lake. Once the ship reaches the other side of the lake, the process goes in reverse and the ship is returned to sea level.

Answer the questions about the reading.

1. The Panama Canal took _____ years to build and opened in _____.

2. An isthmus is a _____.
   a. long strip of land surrounded by water
   b. body of water surrounded and enclosed by land
   c. narrow strip of land bordered on both sides by water
   d. series of lakes and streams that flow into the ocean

3. If a ship once had to travel 14,000 miles to go from New York City to San Francisco, California, and the Panama Canal has reduced this distance to 5,200 miles, how many miles does the ship save? _____

4. The Panama Canal is **not** made up of _____.
   a. 17 artificial lakes   **b.** 3 sets of locks
   c. 9 rivers   **d.** channels

5. The author compares the Panama Canal to a _____
_____.

6. A lock acts like a water slide, and even has a loop. *True* or *false*? _____

7. It takes about _____ hours for a ship to travel through the Panama Canal.

8. You read that the canal shortens the voyage from one side of America to the other. You have experienced that things you need and want to buy are available fairly quickly. Make an inference about how the Panama Canal helps the shipping business.

_____

_____

9. How many ships pass through the Panama Canal each year? _____
   a. about 2,000 ships   **b.** about one million ships
   c. about 100 ships   **d.** about 14,000 ships

10. On a separate sheet of paper, write a few sentences that summarize this reading.

Wow, What a House!

What house has 132 rooms, 35 bathrooms, and receives 6,000 visitors each day? If you're not sure, here's one more hint: the president of the United States and his or her family live there. If you guessed the White House, you're right.

Back in the late 1700s, George Washington, America's first president, decided that the country needed a capital city. He found the perfect spot on the Potomac River, located halfway between the northern and southern states. With the birth of this new place, called Washington, District of Columbia, came elaborate plans for a new city.

Washington, D.C., was once a marshy wilderness filled with wild pigs and mosquitoes. However, after the swamps and creeks were drained, conditions improved and the city began its transformation. City planners decided that a special house would be built for the president. In 1792, bricks, sandstone, and lumber were piled on the north lawn and construction of the White House began.

Although President Washington supervised its construction, he never lived in the White House. John Adams, who was elected the second U.S. president in 1796, was the first president to live there. When he moved in, there were only six finished rooms. Then, almost 18 years later, while President James Madison was living there, British soldiers sailed up the Potomac River and set the White House on fire. Only the outside walls and interior brick walls were left standing. It was rebuilt during the three following years.

The White House has been called many names throughout history. The largest house in the United States until the Civil War, it has been known as the President's Palace, the President's House, and the Executive Mansion. President Theodore Roosevelt gave the White House its official name. That happened in 1901.

Today, the White House is home to the president and his family, as well as many of the people who work and visit there. There are 6 floors, 2 basements, 2 public floors, and 2 floors where the First Family live. The White House has 147 windows, 28 fireplaces, 8 staircases, and 3 elevators. It takes 570 gallons of white paint to cover its outside surfaces.

For the people who live and work there, the White House boasts a tennis court, jogging track, swimming pool, movie theater, billiard room, and bowling alley. Its kitchen can serve dinner to up to 140 people at a time. The five full-time chefs who work there can serve appetizers to more than 1,000 guests at a time!

A trip to Washington, D.C., would not be complete without a tour of this famous landmark.

Answer the questions about the reading.

1. The White House has been given many titles, but President _____ gave the White House its official name.

2. Which U.S. president supervised the construction of the White House but never lived there? _____
    a. President George Washington   **b.** President James Madison
    c. President Theodore Roosevelt   **d.** President John Adams

3. The White House was the largest house in the country until the Civil War. *True* or *false*?

_____

4. Before Washington, D.C., was the country's capital city, it was a marshy wilderness filled with _____ and _____.

5. The White House receives _____ guests each day.
    a. 2,000   **b.** 1,700   **c.** 4,500   **d.** 6,000

6. Using facts from the reading, complete the time line below.

1700s	1792	1796	_____	1901	Today
George Washington established the capital city.	_____ _____ _____ _____ _____ _____	President John Adams moves in.	The White House burns down.	_____ _____ _____ _____ _____ _____	Home to the president, his or her family, and the people who work there.

Hall Monitor in Your Head

A hall monitor walks the halls at school and usually tells people not to go too fast. Monitoring reading comprehension is similar: it's a tiny hall monitor in your head that tells you to adjust your reading rate.

Determining the best reading rate for a certain genre, or type of text, is important. Reading too fast or too slow greatly affects how much or how little you understand of what you read. When you adjust your reading rate, you evaluate the difficulty of the passage you are reading and then act accordingly.

Here is a good rule of thumb: If the sentences are fairly short and there aren't too many unfamiliar words, then a brisk pace is fine. If the passage you are reading is filled with technical vocabulary and complicated explanations, however, then a slower pace is needed.

Place a check next to each sentence that can be read at a normal, brisk, pace. Leave the rest blank.

1. _____ I think the movie was entertaining.

2. _____ Because the shortest distance between two places is a straight line, the bottom part of the wing is shorter in distance than the top, curved part.

3. _____ Your brain weighs about three pounds.

4. _____ Thousands of people of all ages blog each day.

5. _____ Yesterday was my best friend's birthday.

6. _____ Thousands of re-enactors, or men and women who recreate characters from historic events, play the roles of Union and Confederate soldiers.

7. _____ Geochemists, who are scientists who study the chemical changes in the earth's crust, examine radioactive decay to determine the age of a rock.

8. _____ Dinosaurs roamed the earth millions of years ago.

9. _____ My clock stopped in the middle of the night.

10. _____ Without the bitter and strong sensation caused when someone peels an onion, scientists believe that the onion's natural sweet aromas will be the only scent that reaches the nose.

Speed Matters

Now that you know when to read at a normal pace, practice recognizing when to read at a slower or even faster pace.

For example, a sentence like the following should be read at a slower pace because of the complexity of the vocabulary and the length of the sentence:

> Thousands of re-enactors, or men and women who recreate characters from historic events, play the roles of Union and Confederate soldiers.

A sentence like the following can be read much more quickly:

> I love going to the beach with my family.

Write *F* or *S* next to each sentence to tell whether it can be read at a fast or slow pace.

1. _____ The project is still in its beginning stages.

2. _____ My friend is going to Notre Dame.

3. _____ NASA's mission is to lead the way in scientific discovery and aeronautics research.

4. _____ Researchers agreed that the tests were a success.

5. _____ This venting, or action that lets something escape, allows some of the hot air to slowly seep out of the balloon, which lowers the air temperature inside the envelope and causes it to sink toward the ground.

6. _____ My sister loves baked apples.

7. _____ John and Robert Kennedy were brothers.

8. _____ The U.S. Food and Drug Administration works tirelessly to protect the citizens of this nation.

9. _____ Most of the kayaks today are sold to recreational kayakers.

10. _____ I love to play soccer on Saturday mornings.

Soccer and Life

She won the title of U.S. Soccer Female Athlete of the Year award five times. She won Olympic gold and silver medals while playing for America's national soccer team. She is considered the best all-around female soccer player in the world. She is Mia Hamm, and she is a soccer legend.

Born as Mariel Margret Hamm on March 17, 1972, in Selma, Alabama, Mia Hamm grew up in Chapel Hill, North Carolina. In 1994, she graduated from the University of North Carolina with a degree in political science. That was four years after she scored her first goal on the soccer field.

Mia Hamm's accomplishments on and off the soccer field are staggering. Not only was she the youngest ever to play on the U.S. National Soccer Team, but she debuted, or made her first appearance, on the American team when she was only 15 years old.

Mia Hamm's life was impacted by her decision to play soccer as a young girl. She feels fortunate, or lucky, because she was encouraged to play despite her gender and believes that other girls should have the same chance. She believes that her experiences on the soccer field and membership on a team have made her who she is today. On and off the field, Mia Hamm is a superstar.

Called "slashing" and "dynamic," Mia Hamm's soccer style has created a stir. Her winning kicks earned her gold medals in the 1989 and 1990 Olympic Games and a silver medal in 1987. In one of her first Olympic games against the women's soccer team from Sweden, Mia sprained her ankle. She continued to play, however, and helped lead her team to victory that year. But if you ask her what one of her biggest accomplishments is, she will tell you about her foundation.

When her brother, Garrett, died in 1996 from aplastic anemia, a bone marrow disease, Mia Hamm pledged that she would do something to help everyone else who suffered from this condition. As a result, she created the Mia Hamm Foundation. The Mia Hamm Foundation raises money for awareness and research for bone marrow diseases. It also raises funds to encourage and empower girls who want to be athletes. Both bone marrow disease and the support of female athletes are close to Mia's heart. Her dedication and skill on the soccer field is carried over into her work with her foundation.

Answer the questions about the reading.

1. What is the main idea of this reading? ____
    a. Mia Hamm likes to play soccer.
    b. Mia Hamm graduated from college with a political science degree.
    c. Mia Hamm's accomplishments on and off the soccer field are impressive.
    d. Mia Hamm was born in Alabama and moved to North Carolina.

2. Mia Hamm's real name is _____.

3. The word *staggering* in paragraph 3 means? ____
    a. remarkable   **b.** boring   **c.** falling down   **d.** mediocre

4. Mia Hamm won the title of U.S. Soccer Female Athlete of the Year award _____ times.

5. Mia Hamm has been described as "determined." Which sentence from the reading proves this? ____
    a. Mia Hamm's life was impacted by her decision to play soccer as a young girl.
    b. Born as Mariel Margret Hamm on March 17, 1972, in Selma, Alabama, Mia Hamm grew up in Chapel Hill, North Carolina.
    c. She continued to play, however, and helped lead her team to victory that year.
    d. On and off the field, Mia Hamm is a superstar.

6. Something sad happened in Mia's life, and it caused her to act. What happened? ____
    a. She sprained her ankle.   **b.** Her brother died of a bone marrow disease.
    c. She only won two gold medals.   **d.** She was encouraged to play soccer.

7. Number the events in Mia Hamm's life in the correct order.
    ____ Mia Hamm founded the Mia Hamm Foundation.
    ____ Mia Hamm scored her first goal on the soccer field.
    ____ Mia won gold medals at the Olympics in 1989 and 1990.
    ____ She graduated from the University of North Carolina with a degree in political science.

8. Mia Hamm was the youngest person ever to play on the U.S. National Soccer team. *True* or *false*?

_____

Hey, Look, It's a Hybrid!

What do you get when you combine the power of gasoline with the efficiency of electricity? Here's a hint: you can find it on the highway. It's a hybrid!

A hybrid is any vehicle that relies on two sources of power to make it drive. Most hybrid cars on the roads today use a combination of gasoline and electricity. The scientists who created them wanted to ensure that the vehicles do two things: travel farther on less gasoline and do not pollute the air.

Gasoline-powered cars travel at least 300 miles before they need gasoline. It is easy to stop at a gas station and refuel. These cars also do well on the highways. They have no trouble keeping up with traffic. The biggest disadvantages to driving a gasoline-powered car are the cost of gasoline and the large amount of pollution the burned gasoline emits into the environment.

Electric-powered cars, on the other hand, are environment-friendly and produce little to no pollution. But these cars can travel only between 50 and 100 miles before they must recharge their batteries. Recharging is complicated and time-consuming. The car itself also cannot travel as fast as gasoline-powered cars. This puts them at a disadvantage on the highways.

The scientists' solution was to combine the best of both worlds. The result is the hybrid. This gasoline-electric car has six main features. The first is a gasoline engine similar to the one in a gasoline-powered car. It also has a fuel tank, an electric motor, and a generator. A hybrid car generator produces the electrical power to make the car go. The batteries that store that power are another feature of gasoline-electric cars. Finally, like gasoline-powered cars, the hybrid has a transmission.

The key to the hybrid car's efficiency is it's lightweight. Because the car runs on two sources of power, the gasoline engine can be much smaller, which lightens the car. And lighter cars will expend less energy when they go uphill.

Although it is more complicated and expensive to build than a conventional, or regular, automobile, the hybrid car's improved mileage and reduced tailpipe emissions are significant reasons for building it. A car that burns twice as much gasoline to go a mile will also produce twice as much pollution. A hybrid will cut everyday costs and reduce contamination of the air around it.

Answer the questions about the reading.

1. A hybrid is a ____.

    a. car that doesn't need gasoline to run

    b. car that relies on two sources of power to make it drive

    c. vehicle that uses electricity to start

    d. small car that needs to be plugged in at night

2. The most common hybrid on roads today combine _____
and _____ to run.

3. Gasoline-powered cars can travel about 30 miles before they run out of fuel. *True* or *false*?

_____

4. What is so great about hybrid cars? Place a check next to all that apply.

    a. ____ They produce little or no air pollution.

    b. ____ They can only travel up to 100 miles before being recharged.

    c. ____ They cannot travel as fast as gasoline-powered cars.

    d. ____ They are more efficient.

5. The smaller a car's engine is, the more efficient the car is. *True* or *false*? _____

6. Complete the following chart contrasting the gasoline-powered car, the electric-powered car, and the hybrid car.

Gasoline-powered car	Electric-powered car	Hybrid car

This Happened Because of That

The cause is what makes something happen. The effect is what happens.

In the sentence *Emily planted the seeds and a tomato plant grew*, the cause is the act of Emily planting the seeds. The effect is the growth of a tomato plant.

Match each cause to its effect.

Cause

1. _____ The telephone rang.

2. _____ Joseph grabbed his pail and shovel.

3. _____ The fire alarm sounded.

4. _____ The cat yawned.

5. _____ Nicole admired the horse.

6. _____ Christopher loved to read.

7. _____ The snowstorm closed the airport.

8. _____ The big test was the next day.

9. _____ A delivery truck pulled up to the house.

10. _____ Alex's music player stopped.

Effect

a. Michael studied hard.

b. He bought new batteries.

c. A man left a package on the porch.

d. He knew a lot about history.

e. The passengers had to stay on the ground.

f. Her mother bought riding lessons for her.

g. Barbara answered the phone.

h. He fell asleep in the sun.

i. The firefighters jumped in the firetruck.

j. Then he made a sand castle.

The Good and the Bad

Causes are the reasons why effects happen. Effects can be either positive or negative. Look at this example:

Cause: The wind started to blow.

Positive Effect: Our sailboat moved faster across the water.

Negative Effect: Clouds rolled in and rain began to fall.

With a little imagination, you can turn any cause into a good effect or a bad one. Take your best shot!

1. *Cause:* I wore a white shirt to school today.

Positive Effect:_____

Negative Effect:_____

2. *Cause:* My sister borrowed my bike.

Positive Effect:_____

Negative Effect:_____

3. *Cause:* The telephone rang just as I was leaving the house.

Positive Effect:_____

Negative Effect:_____

4. *Cause:* A big moving van parked in front of my neighbors' house.

Positive Effect:_____

Negative Effect:_____

5. *Cause:* Because of the storm, the electricity at my house shut off.

Positive Effect:_____

Negative Effect:_____

A Day in a Play

Characters:

Narrator

Jessica: a thirteen-year-old girl

Thomas: Jessica's twelve-year-old brother

Emily: Jessica's thirteen-year-old cousin

Matt: Jessica's ten-year-old cousin

Scene 1

Scene 1 is set in a small campground in Kentucky. The children are inside their cabin.

NARRATOR: The cousins had been stuck inside their tents for two days because of the drenching rain. The four made the best of this weather by playing cards, listening to their music, and napping. By the third day, the weather has cleared and Jessica, Thomas, Emily, and Matt are ready to shake off their cabin fever and hit the trails.

JESSICA: [standing in the doorway of the cabin that the families shared. She looks out and then back at Emily.] You all set to get going? I can't wait to stretch my legs.

EMILY: Yeah, I'm ready. It just looks so muddy out there.

THOMAS: I agree with Em. I can't stay inside another minute, but I'm not sure I want to hike in all of that mud. It could be dangerous. The other day, the guide warned us about rockslides.

MATT: Nothing will happen. Let's just get going.

NARRATOR: The four throw snacks into backpacks and make sure they have water and emergency medical supplies. Even though Matt's mom and dad plan to tag along, they feel as if they are on their own.

Scene 2

Scene 2 takes place on a well-walked trail in the woods.

JESSICA: This is so great. It's so beautiful out here.

MATT: It really is very muddy, though. Let's follow the trail up the mountain.

EMILY: My feet are getting soaked, but this is much better than sitting in that cabin.

NARRATOR: As the children climb the uphill trail, they hear a rumbling.

THOMAS: Oh, no. That sounds like thunder. Wait, it's rocks rolling down a hill!

JESSICA: Run over here. We need to get off the trail until the rockslide passes.

NARRATOR: The four children and two adults leap off the trail just before three boulders roll down. When the coast is clear, they step carefully back onto the trail.

EMILY: Wait, what was that noise? It sounds like an animal in trouble.

NARRATOR: The group walks a few steps down the trail where they find a small rabbit that appears hurt.

(continued on page 185)

JESSICA: That rabbit must have been hit by one of the boulders. What should we do?

THOMAS: My scout leader told us to call the wildlife ranger if we ever found a wild animal that was hurt. [He turns to his aunt and uncle.] Can you call the ranger's station?

NARRATOR: As the adults get in touch with the wildlife ranger, the children stand back and wait.

MATT: I know I said I didn't want to go hiking in the mud, but I'm sure glad we're here.

Answer the questions about the reading.

1. List the characters in the play: _____

_____

2. What is the setting of the first scene? ____

    a. a trail in the woods   **b.** a cabin in a campground in Kentucky

    c. a mountain top   **d.** a lake along a trail in Maine

3. The narrator of a play describes some of the things that happen. *True* or *false*?_____

4. Do any of the children have scout training? _____ Circle the sentence that is your clue.

5. *The coast is clear* is an idiom. What does it mean? ____

    a. They are out in plain view.   **b.** There are no clouds at the beach.

    c. They are safe now.   **d.** The sky is blue and there are no clouds.

6. On the lines below, write Scene 3. Think about what will happen to the rabbit and how each child will react. Finish on another sheet of paper, if needed.

_____

_____

_____

_____

_____

_____

_____

_____

Iceberrrrrgs Ahead

An iceberg is a large piece of freshwater ice that is floating in open water. The iceberg usually forms by breaking off huge glaciers or ice shelves that were formed by snow. The word *iceberg* is derived from the Dutch word *ijsberg*, which means "ice mountain." An iceberg can range from 3 feet tall to as tall as a 55-story building. But what you see is not what you get. There is a lot more hiding under the sea.

The expression *tip of the iceberg* means that there is more to a problem than meets the eye. The structure of an iceberg and how it looks underwater is the source of that saying. Only about one-ninth of the entire iceberg can be seen above the water The rest is under the sea. The ocean liner *Titanic* was torn open by the jutting, oversized ice chunk that lurked where the crew couldn't see. As a result of this horrible disaster that killed more than 1,500 people, the International Ice Patrol was formed. Before the *Titanic* hit that iceberg in 1912, there was no system for tracking them, and thus no way to warn ships about possible collisions with icebergs. The International Ice Patrol monitors iceberg dangers and lets sailors know of all known icebergs in the waters where they sail.

Icebergs exist in all shapes and sizes. For example, a growler is a small iceberg that is less than 3 feet tall and 16 feet long. A Bergy Bit is a little bigger. Its height ranges from 3 to 13 feet and it can have a length between 15 and 46 feet. An interesting fact about icebergs is that when one melts, it sometimes makes a fizzing sound. That sound, which was named "Bergie Seltzer," occurs when air bubbles are compressed, or pressed together into a smaller space. These air bubbles then become trapped in the iceberg and later make a popping sound when the iceberg melts.

In addition to classifying icebergs by size, the Ice Patrol can identify two classifications, or categories, of icebergs, according to their shape. Tabular icebergs have steep sides and a flat top, like a plateau. Non-tabular icebergs come in all different shapes and sizes. The Ice Patrol uses technology to monitor and identify icebergs. For example, they fly overhead or float buoys with sensors in the water. These drifting icebergs don't move very fast, so to follow one around is not too difficult.

The most important thing to remember about icebergs, though, is that the part you see is just the tip of the iceberg.

Answer the questions about the reading.

1. If the formation of the International Ice Patrol in 1914 is the effect, what was the cause?

_____

2. An iceberg is a(n) ____.

    a. big chunk of saltwater ice floating in the water

    b. large piece of freshwater ice floating in open water

    c. hilly part of a glacier

    d. ice shelf near the Antarctic

3. "The leaky faucet is just the tip of the iceberg," said Uncle Joe. Underline what Uncle Joe means.

    The problem with the faucet is much worse than it looks.

    The leaky faucet is the only thing wrong.

    An iceberg is causing the faucet to leak.

    He wants to fix a leaky faucet.

4. What fraction of an iceberg is under the water? _____

5. What does the International Ice Patrol do? Place a check next to all that apply.

    a. ____ monitor where icebergs are floating   **b.** ____ explore the surfaces of icebergs

    c. ____ classify icebergs by shape and size   **d.** ____ document the history of the *Titanic*

6. A growler is another name for a huge iceberg. *True* or *false*? _____

7. A _____ iceberg has steep sides and a flat top.

8. What does the word *classifications* in paragraph 4 mean? ____

    a. groups of numbers   **b.** number of children in a school

    c. naming things   **d.** categories

9. The sound made by a compressed air bubble releasing from an iceberg is called

    _____.

    Iceberg Pop   Bergie Seltzer   Bergie Bit   Growler

10. The word *iceberg* came from the Dutch word *ijsberg*, which means _____.

Answer Key

Pages 6–7
1. squeezed
2. Answers will vary.
3. possible answers: Max is considerate, sympathetic, and thoughtful. He is creative and wants to help his grandmother.
4. d
5. Max Wallack invented something to help his grandmother and entered it in a contest sponsored by the inventors of Bubble Wrap.
6. b, c
7. possible answers: creativity, usefulness, originality, use of Bubble Wrap
8. possible answers: rap, par, bear, pear, wear, war, babble, blew, blue
9. possible answers: cleverness, resourcefulness, originality, creativity, skill
10. possible answers: call the company, write to the company, check the company's website, research the contest on the Internet

Pages 8–9
1. Barney
2. write
3. Answers will vary.
4. getting a lot of attention
5. d
6. Answers will vary.
7. b, d
8. 48
9. Roosevelt
10. Answers will vary.

Page 10
Paragraphs and headlines will vary.

Page 11
Essays and drawings will vary.

Pages 12–13
1. along the coast of North and South Carolina
2. b
3. eats bugs; secretes a sugary substance
4. leaves
5. eating, devouring, gobbling up, consuming
6. They let the Venus flytrap know something has flown into its leaf.
7. hamburger, pork chop, chicken
8. produce
9. 4, 1, 2, 3, 5
10. Answers will vary.

Pages 14–15
1. Joe
2. The following should be

circled: I love riding in my Uncle Michael's car. During the game, I lean way over my seat after each play to check that my scorebook looks exactly like Uncle Michael's.
3. Monument Park
4. The following should be underlined: Every time I step up to the plate with my bat, I can feel the power building in my swing. It starts at my feet and rises up through my knees and into my arms.
5. center field
6. The following should be circled: Well, center field is waiting for me.
7. Joe dropped his scorebook and touched Mickey Mantle's plaque with his hand.
8. b
9. possible answers: They were surprised, shocked, or unable to explain it.
10. Answers will vary.

Pages 16–17
1. c
2. It curves at the last minute.
3. curveball; The following should be circled: In professional baseball games, the curveball is about 15 miles per hour faster than a fastball.
4. backspin
5. d
6. possible answers: He was a great pitcher. He pitched so well that his arm seemed to be made of gold.
7. a, b, c, e
8. when he or she releases it
9. b
10. true

Pages 18–19
1. 1928
2. It is about real people, places, and events.
3. a
4. rainstorm, sidewalks, Superman, football
5. c
6. Answers will vary.
7. The following should be underlined: The next step is to create a clay model of the balloon.
8. This helps readers understand the story and remember details.
9. c
10. Answers and drawings will vary.

Page 20
Letters will vary.

Page 21
Dialogue will vary.

Pages 22–23
1. b, d
2. read everything they can
3. information
4. c
5. 20 citations $\times$ 52 weeks = 1,040
6. citations
7. d
8. The following should be underlined: Words appearing in their dictionaries reflect the way people live and the words they are using.
9. Answers will vary.
10. Answers will vary.

Pages 24–25
1. d
2. true
3. temporary, fun, enthusiasm
4. 1927
5. possible answer: He was a salesman, so he knew how to sell things. Mr. Dahl is good at selling things, and he is smart and has a good imagination.
6. The following should be circled: salesman; joking around withsome friends; began selling the Pet Rock; a funny manual on how to handle their new pet
7. possible answer: Most fads are things that seem a little silly, like Pet Rocks. People can be enthusiastic about things like that only for certain amounts of time.
8. possible answers: Pez, ant farms, poodle skirts, Frisbees
9. b
10. Answers will vary.

Pages 26–27
1. possible answers: to detect earthquakes and tsunamis; to study sea mammals; to chart the ocean floor
2. b
3. Answers may vary, but may include: read the sound waves; steer the ship; interpret the data
4. true
5. sounds in water; physicist who studies the earth
6. sound waves; pulses; hydrophone
7. the noise disturbs animals and fish that live under the sea
8. Answers may vary, but can include: to find sunken ships;

to discover new sea creatures
9. possible answers: CAT scans are used on people, they help doctors diagnose disease, and they are done in hospitals and doctors' offices; sound waves used by scientists are used underwater, outdoors on ships, and they help scientists see what the ocean floor looks like.
10. c

Pages 28–29
1. Bottled water is convenient and easy to carry around.
2. It makes our bodies slow down and sweat less.
3. dehydrated
4. b
5. Early bottled water was expensive.
6. c
7. 30
8. false
9. Plastic bottles make drinking water easier to do.
10. Answers will vary.

Pages 30–31
1. possible answers: French fries, potato chips, seed potatoes, baked potatoes, boiled potatoes, mashed potatoes
2. a, d
3. spuds, taters, tubers
4. Answers will vary.
5. c
6. Answers will vary.
7. $2.25 $\times$ 11 = $24.75
8. 90 to 100 days
9. b

Page 32
Recipes will vary.

Page 33
Answers will vary.

Pages 34–35
1. The following should be circled: Like the rest of their new home, the garage was built in the early 1900s. They hung the chime on their front porch—a tribute to all the new possibillities and unopened doors that awaited them in their new home.
2. 46 keys
3. d
4. Answers will vary.
5. b
6. possible answers: carefully, excitedly, quickly, slowly
7. Answers will vary.
8. possible answers: They moved

to a new town and didn't know anyone. It was summer vacation.
9. dead bugs
10. false

Pages 36–37
1. prefabricated
2. atmosphere, long counter, booths
3. horse
4. diners
5. Answers will vary, but should retell description of diner.
6. possible answers: French fries, fried eggs, hot dogs, pancakes, club sandwiches, baked potato, tuna salad sandwich
7. Diner names, food, prices, and shorthand will vary.

Pages 38–39
1. Answers will vary.
2. a
3. 6
4. Answers will vary.
5. suggested
6. Something contagious is something that spreads from one person to another.
7. Answers will vary.
8. People yawn for attention.
9. Answers will vary.
10. Answers will vary.

Page 40
Step on no pets; Was it a cat I saw?; Ma has a ham; level; Was it a car or a cat I saw? Nurses run; noon; racecar; kayak

Page 41
Paragraphs and details will vary.

Pages 42–43
1. c
2. facts or information
3. Maine
4. at night
5. b
6. The following should be circled: Aurora borealis are only visible in the northern hemisphere, or the half of Earth between the equator and the North Pole. If you wait long enough and keep looking up in the north sky, your chances of viewing the Northern Lights increase.
7. b, d
8. possible answers: Be patient; make sure the sky is clear.
9. magnetosphere
10. c

Pages 44–45
1. It means he has an equal chance of getting better as he does of getting worse.
2. 1997 – 1971 = 26 years old
3. b
4. when he was 16 years old
5. Answers will vary.

6. The following should be underlined: Throughout his fight against cancer, Lance told everyone that he was going to compete again.
7. strength and determination
8. seven
9. on the Internet, at *www.livestrong.com*
10. Answers will vary.

Pages 46–47
1. makes maps
2. possible answers: Years ago cartographers drew maps by hand, but today cartographers use computers to make maps; years ago a cartographer might need a year to make a map, but today cartographers can do it in one hour.
3. b
4. People will use the map to find their way around.
5. a
6. The following should be underlined: They help people to find places, and they are used to measure distance and plan trips. Some of the maps made by cartographers are used by pilots to find airplane routes and military planners to plan missions.
7. Answers will vary.
8. –10. Maps, legends, and answers will vary.

Pages 48–49
1. lifelong, supermarket
2. Ben and Jerry took an ice cream-making class and opened an ice cream parlor in Vermont.
3. b
4. He has a lot of experience in the food industry.
5. The following should be underlined: After two years of calling and never giving up, John's persistence paid off.
6. cold, creamy confection
7. Answers will vary.
8. c
9. 14
10. Answers will vary.

Pages 50–51
1. c
2. a, b, c
3. possible answers: not afraid of water, brave, friendly
4. Sinbad
5. 10
6. a
7. The author meant that the dogs became companions and friends to the sailors.
8. c
9. Answers will vary.
10. By reading the Coast Guard's website.

Page 52
Questions and answers will vary.

Page 53
Lists will vary, but could include water, food, utensils, matches, sleeping bags, toilet paper, clothes.

Pages 54–55
1. possible answer: At the time, she had been First Lady and was working for the United Nations.
2. b
3. a disease of the spinal cord that causes paralysis
4. possible answer: Since he was paralyzed, he needed her help.
5. 1933
6. The following should be underlined: "No matter how plain a woman may be, if truth and loyalty are stamped upon her face, all will be attracted to her."; faithfulness
7. true
8. b, c, d
9. possible answer: Eleanor was kind, dedicated, intelligent, strong, and loyal.
10. 1962 – 1884 = 78

Pages 56–57
1. any small cake baked in a cup-shaped mold or in a paper baking cup.
2. b, c
3. Answers will vary.
4. One review of her creations stated that the flowers on top of the delicious cupcakes looked like they are blooming from roots underneath the frosting.
5. They were once baked individually and now they can be baked in tins of twelve. They come in more varieties today.
6. because cupcakes remind them of childhood
7. very ornate
8. Answers will vary.
9. true
10. They say it is a fad.

Page 58
Reviews will vary.

Page 59
Answers and speeches will vary.

Pages 60–61
1. b
2. The National Aeronautics and Space Administration, or NASA
3. possible answer: It orbits Earth, photographing and collecting data and images in space.
4. false
5. c
6. data
7. Answers will vary.
8. to collect and store

9. 18 × 8 = 144 hours
10. 200

Pages 62–63
1. b
2. false
3. The cat is happy to see me.
4. The cat is relaxed and friendly.
5. By rubbing their bodies and heads up against their legs

Pages 64–65
1. Web-log
2. b
3. poems, news, thoughts, stories, photos, recipes
4. Answers will vary, but should focus on safety and privacy.
5. Answers will vary.
6. Answers will vary.
7. Yes
8. No
9. They contain up-to-date information. They are good ways to get others' opinions.
10. Answers will vary, but can include things such as likes, dislikes, books and movie recommendations.

Pages 66–67
1. He wanted to show his patriotism to the visiting king and queen. Red, white, and green are the colors of Italy's flag.
2. b
3. immigrant
4. New York City, Chicago
5. d
6. _2_ Spread sauce over the crust.
   _3_ Sprinkle grated mozzarella cheese over the sauce.
   _1_ Flatten the crust into a round or square pan.
   _4_ Add toppings.
7. New York pizza has a thin crust, and Chicago pizza has a thick crust.
8. b
9.

Cause	Effect
Raffaele Esposito wanted to impress the king and queen.	He invented pizza.
Italian immigrants settled in New York City and Chicago.	Small cafes began selling Italian food.

Pages 68–69
1. July 1, 2, and 3, 1863; Civil
2. memorial
3. possible answers: to pay tribute, to learn about history, to honor the soldiers who fought
4. The following should be underlined: Today, thousands of re-enactors, or men and

women who recreate characters from historic events, play the roles of both Union and Confederate soldiers.
5. a, c, d
6. Living history is where people can go to see what life looked like long ago.
7. camp; a place where people set up camp
8. Answers will vary, but should include: visit museums, take a tour, see an encampment
9. Answers will vary.
10. Answers will vary.

Page 70
1. F
2. O
3. F
4. F
5. F
6. O
7. O
8. F
9. F
10. O

Page 71
1. What are you thinking about?
2. woken up in a bad mood
3. do everything he can to win
4. Things don't always turn out the way we want.
5. a person who jokes and is funny

Pages 72–73
1. c
2. to find out what they are composed of; to see how old they are; to learn more about Earth
3. evidence
4. fossils
5. Geiger counter
6. Rocks are much more interesting than fossils.
7. true
8. Rocks and What They Tell Us
9. Yes
10. Every single rock contains a clue about earth's history.

Pages 74–75
1. possible answers: to entertain, to teach a lesson
2. b
3. 4, 1, 3, 2
4. someone who performs or is in a game or show
5. possible answers: She was excited and not paying attention; she couldn't tell the difference between salt and sugar by looking at the canisters, because they looked alike and both salt and sugar are white.
6. possible answers: embarrassed, upset, disappointed
7. c
8.

Cause	Effect
Lisa's mother asked, "Who's our frist contestant?"	The birthday guests started playing Rock Star.
Lisa put salt in the cake instead of sugar.	The cake tasted salty and bitter.

Pages 76–77
1. The following should be circled: The project is in its beginning stages, but it is an exciting one.
2. true
3. b
4. Australia
5. possible answers: They want to make life better for people who love onions; they want to improve the onion's taste.
6. c
7. __4__ Your eyes begin to water.
   __1__ You cut into an onion.
   __2__ The onion produces an oil.
   __3__ An acid in the oil irritates your eyes.
8. Answers will vary.

Pages 78–79
1. city, hub, capital
2. bustling
3. He predicts how much longer the winter will be for the entire country.
4. just around the corner
5. It will happen soon.
6. false
7. b
8. possible answers: all hibernate; are all awakened on February 2
9. a
10. Answers will vary.

Page 80
Sentences will vary.

Page 81
1. like white snow; b
2. as snug as a bug in a rug; b
3. as clean as a whistle; c
4. like a flat pancake; a
5. as solid as a rock; b

Pages 82–83
1. 50
2. b
3.

1958	1969	1981	2000
NASA established by President Eisenhower.	Apollo landed on the moon.	Space Shuttle is launched	International Space Station sent into space.

4. invention
5. true
6. Gemini and Mercury

Pages 84–85
1. true
2. beverage
3. chocolatl
4. c
5. __3__ chocolate bars
   __2__ Tootsie Rolls
   __4__ chocolate kisses
   __1__ first box of chocolates
6. Answers will vary.
7. From bars to bunnies, chocolate seems to keep getting better and better. No wonder more than half of all Americans love it.
8. He thought that if it tasted sweeter more people would drink it.

9. The following should be circled: He experimented with the Aztec's chocolatl by adding sugar to make it sweeter.
10. Answers will vary.

Pages 86–87
1. b
2. 20-pound seabird; pelican
3. false
4. a, b
5. The Flying Fish needed to fly on its own.
6. d
7. true
8. possible answer: They dove underneath it, swam from one side to the other, and played with it.
9. b
10. possible answer: The Flying Fish looked like a pelican.

Page 88
1. c
2. b
3. c
4. b
5. a
6. c

Page 89
1. beau
2. bow
3. counsel
4. council
5. minor
6. miner
7. cue
8. queue
9. current
10. currant

Pages 90–91
1. b
2. d
3. true
4. Ice Age
5. __2__ The *Titanic* sank the next day.
   __4__ The *Titanic* was sailing across the Atlantic Ocean.
   __1__ The *Titanic* hit an iceberg.
   __3__ The *Titanic* set sail in spring of 1912.
6. She doesn't think it is possible to make dinosaurs from DNA.
7. false
8. opinion
9. fact
10. a

Pages 92–93
1. 1400s
2. crossing the Atlantic Ocean
3. true
4. It sailed from 1900 to 1906 and then was grounded near Jamaica.
5. a
6. 3, 2, 4, 1
7. d
8. because jets made air travel more convenient

9. 10
10. Answers will vary.

Pages 94–95
1. b
2. 7,500
3. true
4. The pilot heats the air in the envelope with a propane burner.
5. The hot-air balloon will continue to rise.
6. true
7. Diagram should show and label the envelope, burner, and basket.
8. Drawing will vary.
9. Answers will vary.
10. Answers will vary.

Page 96
Directions will vary.

Page 97
Stories will vary.

Pages 98–99
1. c
2. documentary
3. a, c, d
4. true
5. possible answer: so he can remember details about things that happened in exactly the way they happened
6. c
7. explanation or theory
8. __2__ He studies elephants for a long time.
   __3__ He records everything he sees and experiences.
   __4__ He combines everything that he knows to explain something.
   __1__ He reads as much as he can about elephants.
9. b

Pages 100–101
1. true
2. follow in his brother's footsteps
3. to do the same thing his brother did
4. 1962
5. possible answer: The family probably discussed many things together as they ate.
6. c
7. smart, compassionate, responsible, determined
8. The following should be circled: In March 1968, Robert announced that he would run for President.
9. a, b, d
10. Answers will vary.

Page 102
Designs and titles will vary.

Page 103
Entries will vary.

Pages 104–105
1. b
2. a, d
3. true
4. b
5. The following should be underlined: This rule helps to protect healthy cows from infection.
6. about 200
7. false
8. a
9. d

Pages 106–107
1. c
2. Moving Pictures Expert Group
3. compresses
4. stored
5. listen, enjoy
6. 74
7. 2,000
8. c
9. a
10. Answers will vary.

Page 108
Sentences will vary.

Page 109
Sentences will vary.

Pages 110–111
1. Mom, civic, radar, level, madam
2. b
3. 1950s
4. b, c
5. d
6. a, c
7. easily; silently
8. 1936
9. hunting

Pages 112–113
1. shoes, feet in motion, feeling good.
2. Unstoppable means "unable to be stopped."
3. motion detectors; The following should be circled: They follow the ball.
4. positions a dancer takes
5. Answers will vary, but could be: twisting turning twirls
6. Before they were old, they were new.
7. b, c, d
8. true
9. Answers will vary.
10. Answers will vary.

Pages 114–115
1. symbol
2. 1782
3. b
4. on a two-dollar bill
5. false
6. 1776
7. phrase
8. hope
9. strong and could endure anything
10. The following should be circled: American flag, American bald eagle, Uncle Sam

Page 116
Words and sentences will vary.

Page 117
Comic strips will vary.

Pages 118–119
1. 1600s
2. c
3. false
4. c
5. _4_ The Matterhorn, the first tubular steel coaster, was built at Disneyland.
   _2_ Coney Island opened.
   _3_ Disneyland was created and opened to the public.
   _1_ The Russians invented the roller coaster.
6. They are faster, have more loops, longer drops, and steeper hills.
7. 60
8. true
9. a
10. Answers will vary, but can include: safety features like seatbelts, smooth rails, steep hills, loops, steel rails, drops

Pages 120–121
1. a, b, d
2. water
3. true
4. 3, 1, 4, 2
5. true
6. Yes; The following should be circled: It may seem hard to believe that billions of droplets of water and dust could float, but they do, as long as the air in the cloud is warmer than the air around it.
7. Cirrus cloud
8. Diagrams will vary, but should include wispy cirrus clouds in the high section, storm clouds in the middle section, and stratus and cumulus clouds in the low section.

Page 122
Stamp designs will vary.

Page 123
Press releases will vary.

Pages 124–125
1. b
2. He saw Al Gore's movie and wanted to do something.
3. true
4. possible answers: intelligent, caring, concerned, unselfish, motivated, determined, creative
5. 120, Ventura
6. a, b, d
7. Products sold with less packaging create less waste.
8. c
9. possible answer: Alec seems to feel very strongly about what he and his friends are doing. He believes what they are doing will help.

10. Suggestions may include: write to Alec to show support, make posters for your school, get a group of friends together to do what Alec is doing, read more about global warming

Pages 126–127
1. laws
2. The young animal may not survive when released back into the wild.
3. a, c, d
4. true
5. The following should be circled: It is important to remember, though, never to touch or get close to any wild animal. The best thing to do is let an adult know about your concerns for the animal.
6. b
7. aggravate
8. hurt, sick
9. true
10. to inform or teach

Page 128

Page 129
Word webs will vary.

Pages 130–131
1. 200
2. offshore oil drilling
3. b
4. d
5. a, c
6. by boat or helicopter
7. true
8. possible answer: If many workers stay for weeks, they need someone to cook and fight any fires, among other tasks. Floating oil rigs are where workers live and work.
9. a, b, d
10. Answers will vary.

Pages 132–133
1. because her mother owned it and expected Nicole to walk there after school every day
2. false
3. d
4. a, b, c
5. patient and creative
6. b
7. true
8. Endings will vary.

Page 134
Lists will vary.

Page 135
Paragraphs and dialogue will vary.

Pages 136–137
1. 81 percent
2. 81

3. a, b, c
4. television news programs
5. false
6. Bars should be: 81% for television; 50% for newspapers; 44% for radio; 25% for Internet
7. Television is the most popular way people get their news.
8. Answers will vary.

Pages 138–139
1. 3,500
2. b
3. true
4. a
5. Junior Chamber of Commerce of Rockland; parade, concert, coronation ball
6. Yes; The following should be circled: community leaders rallied, or came together to show their support, and reorganized the event.
7. c
8. a, b, c
9. false

Page 140
Haikus and drawings will vary.

Page 141
Cinquains will vary.

Pages 142–143
1. Nintendoitis
2. a
3. false
4. b
5. The following should be circled: Pressing repeatedly on the buttons on a video game controller caused the tendons in the thumbs to become irritated.
6. Take a break and put ice on it.
7. d
8. true
9. Answers will vary, but ad should include: use BlackBerry less, talk on the phone instead of texting, and turn the BlackBerry off.
10. Advertisements will vary.

Pages 144–145
1. true
2. 17,000
3. b
4. a, c, d
5. 3, 1, 2, 4
6. true
7. safer
8. b
9. small
10. Answers will vary.

Page 146
Paragraphs will vary.

Page 147
Paragraphs will vary.

Pages 148–149
1. c
2. weatherperson
3. true
4. a
5. sensible temperature
6. false
7. d
8. Yes; The following should be circled: Knowing the wind chill can help you dress so that, when you do go out, you can feel warm and enjoy your time safely.
9. frostbite, hypothermia
10. Answers will vary.

Pages 150–151
1. Secretary of State
2. a, b, d
3. She wasn't allowed to go into an amusement park because of her race.
4. true
5. possible answer: Black people were treated unfairly during the 1960s because of the color of their skin.
6. c
7. Yes; The following should be underlined: In her free time, Condoleezza managed to continue to play the piano.
8. Paragraphs will vary.

Page 152
1. F
2. F
3. T
4. F
5. T

Page 153
Paragraphs will vary.

Pages 154–155
1. Daniel Bernoulli
2. true
3. b
4. a bird
5. a
6. a, b, d
7. by illustrating it with a piece of cardboard and wind
8. movement, lift, drag
9. c

Pages 156–157
1. a, b, d
2. true
3. carried messengers and equipment, pulled wagons and ambulances, transported generals
4. muscular, strong, dedicated, sturdy

5. b, c, d
6. false
7. possible answers: they could spot potential dangers from atop a horse; they could monitor their troops
8. Traveler
9. c
10. Answers will vary.

Page 158
1. Kim's smile is as [sweet as candy].
2. My dog is big, but he is as [gentle as a lamb].
3. My teacher told us that taking drugs is like [playing with fire].
4. The boy's temper was as [explosive as fireworks].
5. The bad news hit me like a [ton of bricks].
6. M
7. M
8. S
9. M
10. S

Page 159
1. My alarm clock told me it was time to get up.
2. The sunlight danced on the windowsill.
3. My mother's car coughed and sputtered when she started it.
4. The light rain kissed my face as I walked home.
5. I heard the wind whispering in the trees.
6. S
7. P
8. P
9. S
10. M
11. S
12. P
13. P
14. S
15. P

Pages 160–161
1. true
2. processing information
3.

neurons ——— a chemical released by the brain
axons ——— brain cells
neurotransmitter ——— a chemical causing feelings of pleasure
dopamine ——— tiny branches connected to neurons

4. false
5. dopamine
6. b
7. true
8. depressed
9. drug addiction
10. Answers will vary.

Pages 162–163
1. Center Falls
2. excited
3. hopeful, friendly, outgoing, motivated

4. true
5. b
6. a
7. a group of cats that lived in a barn
8. Yes. The following should be circled: Kelly was relieved to see some friendly faces.
9. possible answers: People might not understand what's expected of them; a script tells the actors what to do and say.
10. Answers will vary.

Page 164
Diagrams will vary.

Page 165
Paragraphs will vary.

Pages 166–167
1. c
2. police officers
3. c
4. proof
5. false
6. _3_ The crime scene investigator takes photographs and draws sketches.
_4_ The evidence is sent to the crime laboratory.
_1_ The crime scene investigator does an initial walk through without touching anything.
_2_ Detectives interview people at the crime scene.
7. He or she sees the judge if a search warrant is needed.
8. a

Pages 168–169
1. 1959
2. a, b
3. b
4. true
5. 3, 2, 1, 4
6. 4,000; 120
7. a
8. possible answers: they are good students; they have strong problem solving skills, motivation, experience, and the ability to adapt
9. The voyage into space begins with a dream.

Page 170
Essays will vary.

Page 171
Lists and letters will vary.

Pages 172–173
1. 10; 1914
2. c
3. 14,000 − 5,200 = 8,800 miles
4. c
5. two-lane highway made of water
6. false
7. nine
8. possible answer: They are able to ship their products more efficiently because the trip is shorter.
9. d
10. Summaries will vary.

Pages 174–175
1. Theodore Roosevelt
2. a
3. true
4. wild pigs, mosquitoes
5. d
6.

1700s	1792	1796	1814	1901	Today
George Washington established the capital city.	Construction of the White House begins	President John Adams moves in.	The White House burns down.	President Theodore Roosevelt gives the White House its official name.	Home to the president, his or her family, and the people who work there.

Page 176
1. ✓
2.
3. ✓
4. ✓
5. ✓
6.
7.
8. ✓
9. ✓
10.

Page 177
1. F
2. F
3. S
4. F
5. S
6. F
7. F
8. S
9. S
10. F

Pages 178–179
1. c
2. Mariel Margret Hamm
3. a
4. five
5. c
6. b
7. _4_ Mia Hamm founded the Mia Hamm Foundation.
_1_ Mia Hamm scored her first goal on the soccer field.
_3_ Mia won gold medals at the Olympics in 1989 and 1990.
_2_ She graduated from the University of North Carolina

with a degree in political science.
8. true

Pages 180–181
1. b
2. gasoline, electricity
3. false
4. a, d
5. true
6. Under gasoline powered car: goes 300 miles before refueling; easy to refuel; good on highways; gasoline is expensive; pollution; Under electric-powered car: can only go up to 100 miles before recharging; does not go that fast on highways; does not pollute; Under hybrid: more fuel efficient; can keep up with traffic; does not pollute the environment; more expensive than a conventional car

Page 182
1. g
2. j
3. i
4. h
5. f
6. d
7. e
8. a
9. c
10. b

Page 183
Positive and negative effects will vary.

Pages 184–185
1. Narrator, Jessica, Thomas, Emily, Matt
2. b
3. true
4. Yes, Thomas; The following should be circled: My scout leader told us to call the wildlife ranger if we ever found a wild animal that was hurt.
5. c
6. Scenes will vary.

Pages 186–187
1. the sinking of the Titanic after it hit an iceberg
2. b
3. The problem with the faucet is much worse than it looks.
4. eight-ninths
5. a, c
6. false
7. tabular
8. d
9. Bergie Seltzer
10. ice mountain